COMPACT *Research*

HPV

Peggy J. Parks

Diseases and Disorders

ReferencePoint
Press™

San Diego, CA

© 2009 ReferencePoint Press, Inc.

For more information, contact:
ReferencePoint Press, Inc.
PO Box 27779
San Diego, CA 92198
www.ReferencePointPress.com

Picture credits:
Maury Aaseng: 31–34, 47–49, 63–66, 80–83
AP Images: 17
Landov: 11

LIBRARY OF CONGRESS CATALOGING-IN-PUBLICATION DATA

Parks, Peggy J., 1951–
  HPV / by Peggy J. Parks.
    p. cm. — (Compact research)
  Includes bibliographical references and index.
  ISBN-13: 978-1-60152-070-8 (hardback)
  ISBN-10: 1-60152-070-0 (hardback)
  1. Papillomaviruses. 2. Papillomavirus diseases. I. Title.
  RC168.P15P366 2008
  362.196'911—dc22
                                                          2008044026

Contents

Foreword

As modern civilization continues to evolve, its ability to create, store, distribute, and access information expands exponentially. The explosion of information from all media continues to increase at a phenomenal rate. By 2020 some experts predict the worldwide information base will double every 73 days. While access to diverse sources of information and perspectives is paramount to any democratic society, information alone cannot help people gain knowledge and understanding. Information must be organized and presented clearly and succinctly in order to be understood. The challenge in the digital age becomes not the creation of information, but how best to sort, organize, enhance, and present information.

ReferencePoint Press developed the *Compact Research* series with this challenge of the information age in mind. More than any other subject area today, researching current issues can yield vast, diverse, and unqualified information that can be intimidating and overwhelming for even the most advanced and motivated researcher. The *Compact Research* series offers a compact, relevant, intelligent, and conveniently organized collection of information covering a variety of current topics ranging from illegal immigration and methamphetamine to diseases such as anorexia and meningitis.

The series focuses on three types of information: objective single-author narratives, opinion-based primary source quotations, and facts and statistics. The clearly written objective narratives provide context and reliable background information. Primary source quotes are carefully selected and cited, exposing the reader to differing points of view. And facts and statistics sections aid the reader in evaluating perspectives. Presenting these key types of information creates a richer, more balanced learning experience.

For better understanding and convenience, the series enhances information by organizing it into narrower topics and adding design features that make it easy for a reader to identify desired content. For example, in *Compact Research: Illegal Immigration*, a chapter covering the economic impact of illegal immigration has an objective narrative explaining the various ways the economy is impacted, a balanced section of numerous primary source quotes on the topic, followed by facts and full-color illustrations to encourage evaluation of contrasting perspectives.

The ancient Roman philosopher Lucius Annaeus Seneca wrote, "It is quality rather than quantity that matters." More than just a collection of content, the *Compact Research* series is simply committed to creating, finding, organizing, and presenting the most relevant and appropriate amount of information on a current topic in a user-friendly style that invites, intrigues, and fosters understanding.

HPV at a Glance

Defining HPV

The human papillomavirus, or HPV, is often referred to in the singular form, but it is not just one virus; rather, it comprises a group of over 100 related viruses, each of which has been assigned a number known as an HPV type or strain.

Types of HPV

HPVs are classified as low-risk (wart causing) or high-risk (cancer causing); some HPVs are much more infectious than others.

HPV Infection

HPVs are different from other viruses in that they solely infect the skin rather than the blood, bones, or internal organs. Instead, HPVs enter either the cutaneous (visible) skin that covers the outside of the body, or the mucosal skin, which is the warm, skin-like layers that line the inside of the mouth, as well as the vagina, anus, head of the penis, and other cavities that open to the outside of the body.

Prevalence

The American Medical Association states that more than 440 million people worldwide are infected with HPV, including an estimated 20 million in the United States.

Causes of Genital HPV Infection

By far, the most common cause of HPV infection is sexual intercourse (either vaginal or anal), but cases of infection have been reported that involved sex-play with no penetrative intercourse.

Awareness

Studies have shown that awareness of HPV is disproportionately low compared to more well-known viruses such as HIV; even health-care professionals have been shown to lack adequate knowledge about the epidemic and how serious it is.

Symptoms and Health Risks

Although most people do not develop any symptoms of HPV infection, those who do typically have warts on various areas of the body, depending on which HPV strain they are infected with. The health risks range from cervical cancer in women to other forms of cancer (oral, anal) in men as well as women.

Diagnosis and Treatment

As with all viruses, a cure for HPV infection does not exist; however, warts can be treated with various methods (including cryotherapy), and cancer, if caught early enough, can be treated with radiation and chemotherapy.

HPV Vaccination

As of October 2008 Gardasil was the only HPV vaccine approved by the FDA; it protects against 2 high-risk strains of HPV that cause 70 percent of cervical cancer cases, and 2 low-risk types that have been associated with 90 percent of genital warts. As of November 2008, Gardasil was approved only for girls and young women aged 9 to 26 and not for males, but studies are in progress to determine its effectiveness and safety for older women and males.

Overview

A rianna Daut was 21 years old when she learned that she had been infected with the human papillomavirus, or HPV. She had recently moved from her native Utah to Arizona to begin her career as an illustrator, and before long she met a young man to whom she was very attracted. Daut, who at the time was a virgin, moved in with him and became involved in her first sexual relationship. Because she had been raised in a conservative, religious home where sex was not discussed, she knew very little about sexually transmitted diseases and had never even heard of HPV. Two months later she developed mysterious, painful genital sores that she describes as "red, dime-sized blisters, with clear fluid draining from them. It hurt to touch them and even to walk or pee." She also found painless white bumps scattered across her vulva (the area outside the vagina). She was scared, but hoping it was nothing more than an allergic reaction to a new laundry soap, Daut went to the doctor and was tested. The results showed that she was infected with not only HPV, but also the herpes virus. She was ashamed and embarrassed as well as shocked, because she had been intimate with only one man, and he had obviously passed along the sexually transmitted infections to her. The doctor's insensitive, unhelpful attitude further added to her misery. "Why me?" she wondered. "In the days that followed, my self-esteem plunged. Because of my upbringing, I couldn't help thinking the STDs were punishment for having sex before marriage."[1]

Daut underwent laser surgery to remove the warts from inside her vagina, as well as those that the doctor discovered on her cervix, and she used an acid-based topical solution to treat the visible warts. After she had finished the treatments, she assumed that she was cured, but a follow-up Pap test showed cancerous cells had developed on her cervix—which meant she was at risk for developing cervical cancer. "I was terrified," she writes. "I honestly thought I was going to die."[2] Daut went through more rounds of laser surgery to remove the cancerous cells from her cervix and she is now cancer free. She will, however, have to be vigilant about getting routine checks because she is aware that the cancer could come back at any time. "It sounds crazy," she writes, "but the main thing I regret is wasting all that time feeling ashamed and dirty. What happened to me was unlucky, yes, but I'm no longer plagued by the idea that I brought it on myself."[3]

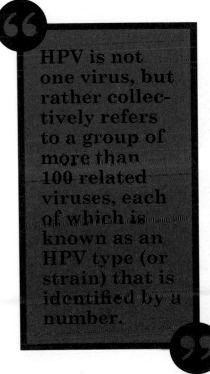

"HPV is not one virus, but rather collectively refers to a group of more than 100 related viruses, each of which is known as an HPV type (or strain) that is identified by a number.

What Is HPV?

HPV is not one virus, but rather collectively refers to a group of more than 100 related viruses, each of which is known as an HPV type (or strain) that is identified by a number. These numbers have been assigned throughout the years in the order in which researchers have discovered the viruses. The term "papilloma" is used to describe the viruses because a number of HPVs cause papillomas, which are actually small benign tumors more commonly known as warts. HPVs are only attracted to, and live in, certain cells of the body: the thin, flat cells known as squamous epithelial cells, or cells that are found on the epithelium (the medical term for skin). Squamous epithelial cells are on the surface of the skin, mouth, and throat in males and females; in the cervix, vagina, anus, and vulva in females; and in the anus, scrotum, and head of the penis in males. According to the American Cancer Society, HPVs are different from other viruses because they do not grow in other parts of the body.

What Causes HPV Infection?

Although HPVs are contagious, not all people who come in contact with them become infected because their immune systems fight the viruses off. People can catch the most common types through physical contact with others who have visible warts, or by touching objects used by someone who has warts on their hands, feet, or other areas of the body.

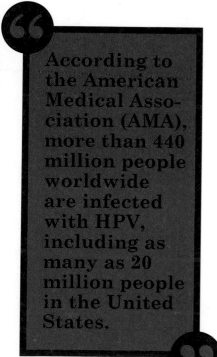

According to the American Medical Association (AMA), more than 440 million people worldwide are infected with HPV, including as many as 20 million people in the United States.

Genital HPV, which is highly contagious, is most commonly passed through sexual intercourse, vaginal as well as anal. It has also been shown to be transmitted through genital to genital contact in the absence of intercourse, as well as through oral sex. But it can also be transmitted in other ways, as researcher Diane M. Harper explains: "HPV is a skin-to-skin infection. Although . . . HPV is most often associated with sexual activity, HPV is not just spread through sex. We have multiple papers where that's documented. We know that 3-year-olds, 5-year-olds, 10-year-olds, and women who have never had sex have been found to be positive for the cancer-causing HPV types."[4]

How Common Is Genital HPV?

Of all the sexually transmitted infections that exist, HPV is by far the most prevalent, as the American Cancer Society explains: "Genital HPV

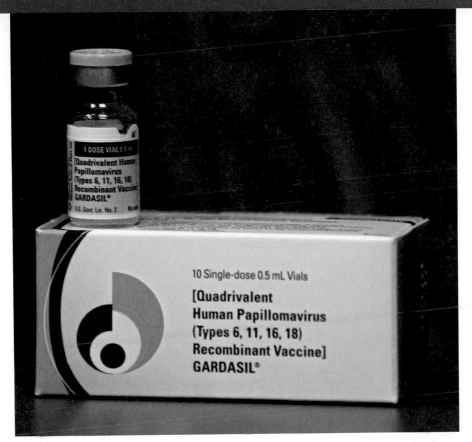

As of October 2008 Gardasil was the only HPV vaccine approved by the FDA. It protects against 2 high-risk strains of HPV that cause 70 percent of cervical cancer cases, and 2 low-risk types that have been associated with 90 percent of genital warts.

is a very common virus. Some doctors think it is almost as common as the common cold virus."[5] According to the American Medical Association (AMA), more than 440 million people worldwide are infected with HPV, including as many as 20 million people in the United States. The American Cancer Society offers the bleak prediction that as many as three-fourths of the people who have ever had sex will be infected by genital HPV at some point during their lifetimes.

Symptoms of HPV Infection

When symptoms of HPV infection are visible, they often appear in the form of warts that grow on various parts of the body. Different types of HPV can result in genital warts in both men and women, although not all infected individuals develop warts. In fact, the biggest reason why genital HPV is so common and spreads so readily is that most people who have it develop no symptoms and are unaware that they have been infected—which means they can spread the virus without knowing it. The American Social Health Association explains: "While the vast majority of sexually active Americans are estimated to have HPV at some point in their lives, most are never diagnosed clinically and remain unaware they were even exposed."[6]

Who Is at Risk for Getting HPV?

According to the Mayo Clinic, the primary risk factor for HPV infections that cause common warts, plantar warts, and flat warts, is young age. The group explains: "Children and adolescents are more likely to be vulnerable to these HPV infections than are adults."[7] Health experts are not certain why warts affect younger people most often, but one factor could be that their immune systems are not yet fully developed. Also, children frequently suffer cuts and scratches, which provide an ideal way for the virus to enter their bodies once they have been exposed to it. Studies have shown that children who bite their nails or pick at hangnails have a higher frequency of warts than those who do not.

Age is also a contributing factor in genital HPV infections, which are most common in sexually active adolescent girls and women aged 15 to 25. The Mayo Clinic states that while the risk may be attributed to increased sexual activity of people in this age group, research has suggested that younger women may also be biologically more vulnerable to the virus than older women. But contrary to what is often believed, genital HPV infection is not necessarily a sign that someone has slept around or had sex with numerous partners. "It's not about promiscuity," says Anna R. Giuliano, who is a professor of medicine and epidemiology at the H. Lee Moffitt Cancer Center and Research Institute in Tampa, Florida. "The more we can get that out of people's minds, the faster we'll be able to get prevention efforts out there. I worry that people will say, 'Oh that's not me, it's not something I have to worry about.'"[8] The reality is, anyone who has sexual relations—even just one time—is at risk of contracting HPV infection.

Yet even though HPV infection can occur after a single sexual encounter, males and females who have multiple sex partners, or who have sex with someone who has had many sex partners, have a higher risk of being infected. Pediatrician Margaret J. Meeker explains: "Every time a person has sex with someone, it is like having sex with every person your partner has ever been with. This is an astounding concept but it is true. Most young people do not think it can happen to them . . . it is not surprising that the number of infected youth is so high."[9]

What Are the Health Risks of Genital HPV Infection?

Genital HPVs are usually categorized as either low risk (wart causing) or high risk (cancer causing). Of the estimated 40 HPVs that can infect the genital area, types 6 and 11 are responsible for about 90 percent of genital warts, which are not cancerous. In many cases these HPVs are naturally inactivated by the body's immune system, which means the virus eventually becomes dormant and the infected cells return to normal. Studies have shown that about 70 percent of new HPV infections disappear within one year, and 90 percent disappear within 2 years.

High-risk HPV infections may also be cleared by the immune system, but this is not as common as with low-risk types. High-risk HPVs have been known to linger in the body for many years, often undetected because no symptoms become apparent. Over time they can cause normal cells in infected areas to turn abnormal and potentially become cancerous. Scientists now know that nearly 100 percent of cervical cancer cases are caused by infection with high-risk HPV, with an estimated 70 percent caused by HPV types 16 or 18. Cervical cancer, which is the third leading cause of cancer death among women worldwide, does not exhibit symptoms until it is quite advanced. As a result, each year more than 240,000 women throughout the world die of cervical cancer, and most of them live in developing countries where diagnostic tests are often not available.

> Age is also a contributing factor in genital HPV infections, which are most common in sexually active adolescent girls and women aged 15 to 25.

Cervical cancer, however, is not the only type of cancer that can be caused by high-risk HPV infection. According to the Centers for Disease

Control and Prevention (CDC), in some cases HPV infection can also lead to oral cancer in both men and women; cancer of the vulva, vagina, and anus in women; and cancer of the penis and anus in men. The CDC adds that gay and bisexual men are 17 times more likely to develop cancer of the anus than heterosexual men. A young gay man who wrote anonymously in the November 2005 issue of *AIDS Treatment Update* shared his personal experience with anal cancer. After he was diagnosed, he had several surgeries to remove large cancerous warts from his anus and suffered through months of excruciating pain. "I could barely walk for hours after using the toilet," he writes, "and I was in tears most days."[10] After his treatment the doctors could find no evidence of any cancerous cells, and this was a relief. He is still fearful about the future, however, as he explains: "I'm still worked up about whether I might end up with cancer one of these days, or even that the warts will return and require more surgery. But what scares me the most is that the experts still don't know the best way to prevent progression from warts to pre-cancer to cancer— maybe they will have worked it out in ten years, but for me, right now, the uncertainty is difficult to deal with."[11]

> Genital HPVs are usually categorized as either low risk (wart causing) or high risk (cancer causing).

Diagnosis and Treatment

Although no cure exists for HPV, it can be diagnosed and treated in various ways. Physicians can usually diagnose common, plantar, and other nongenital warts based on a physical examination. Most warts do not require treatment, but people often choose to treat them because they can be painful, annoying, and can also spread to other parts of the body. These warts can be treated through a process known as cryotherapy, in which extremely cold liquid nitrogen destroys the warts by freezing them. Another somewhat unusual treatment is known as duct tape therapy. It involves covering the wart with a small piece of duct tape and leaving the tape in place for 6 days. On the seventh day the tape is removed, the area is soaked in water, and then the wart is scraped with an emery board or pumice stone. The wart is left bare for one night, and the next day the process is started over again. This process continues for about 2 months or until the wart has disappeared. According to a study performed by researchers in 2002, the warts of 22 patients (85 percent of 26) who underwent duct tape therapy disappeared, compare to 15 patients (60 percent of 25) whose warts were treated with cryotherapy.

As with common warts, genital warts also can usually be diagnosed by visual examination. To confirm the diagnosis, the physician may apply a vinegar solution to the genital area, which turns HPV-infected areas white and makes them more visible. The warts can be treated in various ways, some of which are topical medications, chemical treatments that burn off the warts, cryotherapy, surgical removal, or laser surgery. Yet even if no visible signs of genital HPV infection exist, the American Cancer Society recommends that women over the age of 30 have not only an annual Pap test but also a DNA test for HPV. Such tests have been shown to detect 13 of the most common types of high-risk HPV types and have detected precancerous lesions that did not show up on Pap tests.

Can Genital HPV Infection Be Prevented?

The only sure way to prevent genital HPV infection is total abstinence from sex. Laura Koutsky, who is a professor and HPV expert at Seattle's University of Washington, shares her thoughts: "It's really pretty impossible to avoid acquiring one or more genital HPV infections if you decide you're going to be sexually active in your life. If we lock ourselves up in the house and don't associate with people, we won't get colds. If you never have sex, you won't get HPV. It's not clear we want to live that way."[12]

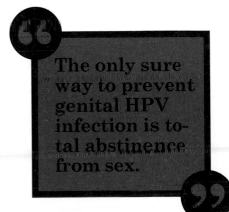

The only sure way to prevent genital HPV infection is total abstinence from sex.

People can take steps, however, to reduce their risk of getting HPV, such as limiting the number of their sex partners and choosing partners who have had few or no prior sexual encounters. Latex condoms can provide some protection against HPV, but not 100 percent protection because they do not cover the entire genital area of either partner, such as the vulva, anus, base of the penis, and scrotum. These areas may be teeming with infectious viruses, and as a result, HPVs can be spread when the areas come into contact with unprotected skin. Meeker explains: "In 2001, the U.S. National Institutes for Health reviewed the best medical literature available on how well condoms 'work.' Their results were not widely publicized but are astonishing. They found that for . . . infections like herpes and HPV (human papilloma virus), which are transmitted from skin to skin, condoms fare extremely poorly."[13]

Should the HPV Vaccine Be Mandatory?

In June 2006 a vaccine called Gardasil was approved by the U.S. Food and Drug Administration (FDA) for adolescent girls and young women. Whether this vaccination should be required by law for young girls is an issue of heated controversy. Although organizations such as Concerned Women for America (CWA) are in favor of the vaccine, they are adamantly against making it mandatory because they believe the decision to vaccinate belongs with parents rather than the government. Others oppose the vaccine altogether, saying that it could encourage young girls to become promiscuous at a young age. That is the perspective of Tony Perkins, who is president of the conservative Christian group Family Research Council. In 2005 Perkins publicly stated that he had no intention of getting his 13-year-old daughter vaccinated because she would then be inclined to have sex before she was married. "It sends the wrong message," Perkins said. "Our concern is that this vaccine will be marketed to a segment of the population that should be getting a message about abstinence."[14]

People who disagree with Perkins believe that any vaccine capable of preventing deadly viral infections that cause cancer should be as high of a priority as childhood vaccines for mumps, measles, smallpox, diphtheria, tetanus, and polio. Journalist Nancy Gibbs, who has a young daughter, refutes the vaccine/promiscuity connection by using an analogy: "When my 11-year-old got her tetanus shot during her checkup last week, her pediatrician did not tell her that it was now safe to go dance barefoot on rusty nails." Gibbs quips about what doctors will *not* say as they are administering the vaccine: "'There! Now when you go out and have promiscuous, unprotected intercourse with strangers, at least there is one less sexually transmitted disease to worry about.' I think they're much

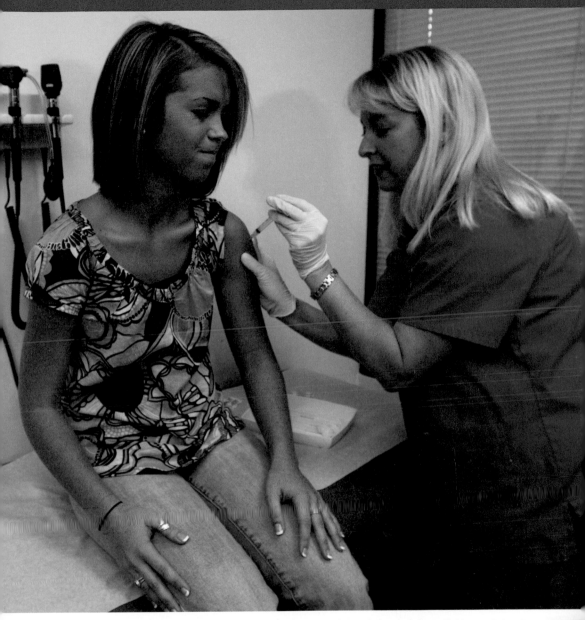

This 18-year-old winces as she has her third and final dose of the HPV vaccine. Whether this vaccination should be required by law for young girls is an issue of heated controversy.

more likely to say, 'This will only hurt for a second.'"[15] To decrease the incidence of HPV infection, and hopefully reduce the risk of cervical cancer in young women, a number of states are considering legislation that would make the vaccine mandatory.

HPV in the Future

HPVs pose a serious problem in the United States as well as throughout the world. More than 100 types of these viruses are infectious, extremely common, and easily spread from one person to another. Skin warts caused by HPV can be painful and annoying, but they are not life threatening, and the same is true of genital warts. But high-risk HPVs can lead to severe problems such as abnormal cells that cause cervical cancer in women, as well as other types of cancers that afflict both women and men. Thus far the HPV vaccination is recommended only for women under the age of 26, and it is not available for men. Yet even though it can protect against most of the HPVs that cause cervical cancer, it does not prevent all HPV infection. So what can be done to stop this HPV epidemic? Is it even possible to stop it? Hopefully, as researchers continue to study HPV, they will come up with answers to those critical questions. Until then, it will continue to be a problem that affects people everywhere—no matter their age, race, or gender.

What Is HPV?

> **Human papillomavirus, or HPV, is a collective term for approximately 100 types of viruses, some of which lead to abnormal growths or cell changes. Warts (e.g., plantar warts, warts on the tongue or tonsils) . . . are benign growths on the skin or mucous membranes that are caused by HPV.**

—Stanley J. Swierzewski, "HPV and Vaccination."

> **Approximately 20 million Americans are currently infected with HPV, and another 6.2 million people become newly infected each year. At least 50% of sexually active men and women acquire genital HPV infection at some point in their lives.**

—Centers for Disease Control and Prevention (CDC), "Genital HPV."

In 1933 Richard E. Shope, a renowned American physician from Iowa, made a discovery that was later hailed as one of the most important scientific findings in HPV research. Shope, who had made a name for himself as an expert who specialized in animal viral diseases, had become interested in a skin condition that afflicted wild, cottontail rabbits in Iowa and Kansas. Hunters reported on the unusual condition of the rabbits, which, as Shope wrote, "were said to have numerous horn-like protuberances on the skin over various parts of their bodies. The animals were referred to popularly as 'horned' or 'warty' rabbits."[16] Shope obtained shipments of wild and tame cottontails for his own research and began to closely study those that had papillae, the scientific term for wart-like growths. He found that the most common sites of the warts were on the rabbits' inner thighs, abdomens, necks, and shoulders. The growths were black or grayish black in color, and when cut open they had white or pinkish-white, fleshy centers. Shope found that when he rubbed material from the warts on the shaved, lightly abraded skin of uninfected rabbits, warts began to appear on the site after 6 to 12 days. The warts were loosely attached to the skin so they came off easily when the animals were handled. The areas often bled but usually healed without complication, although in some cases new warts grew back in the same site. Shope concluded that warts were caused by the papillomavirus, and he had proven that the virus was contagious and could be spread among animals. He wrote about his findings in a paper entitled "Infectious Papillomatosis of Rabbits," which was published in the July 19, 1933, issue of the *Journal of Experimental Medicine*. Shope's concluding summary stated: "A papilloma has been observed in wild cottontail rabbits and has been found to be transmissible to both wild and domestic rabbits."[17]

Two years later scientists Peyton Rous and J.W. Beard, who continued to pursue Shope's studies with rabbits, made another crucial discovery. They found that when the animals' warts were allowed to grow unchecked, some of the growths eventually became malignant. This was a monumental finding because, for the first time, research had clearly shown a relationship between the papillomavirus and at least some forms of cancer. It would be decades, however, before scientists discovered that the virus affected humans in the same way.

Viruses and HPV Types

In order to understand HPV, it is important to know what viruses are and how they function. The word *virus* comes from the Latin word of the same spelling that connotes something that is poisonous or venomous. Each viral particle (known as a virion) is a microscopic fragment of nucleic acid, such as deoxyribonucleic acid (DNA) or ribonucleic acid (RNA) that is enclosed in a shell of protein. Viruses are unbelievably tiny—about a thousand times smaller than bacteria—so small, in fact, that they can be seen only with special electron microscopes. Unlike cells and bacteria, which have the ability to reproduce and multiply, viruses do not contain the chemical enzymes that are essential for reproduction.

Instead, they are molecular parasites that attack and invade living "host" cells, which they use as factories to carry out reproduction by generating more and more viral material. Science writer Corey Binns explains: "Viruses prey upon all living organisms, turning them into virus Xerox machines. Unlike a bacterium or a cell of an animal, a virus lacks the ability to replicate on its own. A virus does contain some genetic information critical for making copies of itself, but it can't get the job done without the help of a cell's duplicating equipment, borrowing enzymes and other molecules to concoct more virus."[18] Once viruses have entered the body, they hunt for their specific type of host cell to infect. Cells that have been hijacked by a virus eventually die and burst apart, freeing the virus particles to scatter and attack other cells in the body. One par-

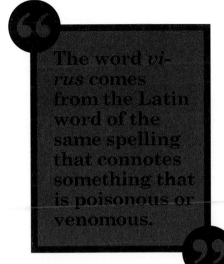

The word *virus* comes from the Latin word of the same spelling that connotes something that is poisonous or venomous.

ticularly obvious example of this phenomenon is cold sores, which are caused by the herpes simplex virus. A cold sore, which often appears on the lips, is the area of dead tissue where the virus attacked and killed cells, causing them to burst open.

According to HPV expert and physician Joel Palefsky, HPVs attack different areas of the body depending on the specific type, as he explains: "HPV is particular. . . . Not only does it only hang out in its own species (humans), but each of the more than one hundred HPV types has its own favorite hangout in the skin of the human body. . . . Some like the hands and feet, and some like the genital region. They rarely, if ever, cross over!"[19] The most common symptoms of HPV infection are various types of warts. Plantar warts, which are often mistaken for corns or calluses, tend to develop on the heels or balls of the feet, the areas that feel the most pressure. They may appear as small, fleshy bumps or hard, flat growths, and if not treated they may multiply and spread into clusters known as mosaic warts. Common warts, which tend to grow on the hands and feet, typically have a raised surface with a cauliflower-like head, while flat warts have a flattened appearance and usually develop on the face, neck, hands, wrists, elbows, or knees.

Certain types of HPV can cause warts in the genital areas in both men and women. These genital warts may be small red or white bumps; tiny, cauliflower-like clusters; or flat, flesh-colored bumps that are barely visible. In women, genital warts may grow on the lips of the vulva, around the clitoris, in and around the anus, and on the linings of the vagina, cervix, and rectum. In men, genital warts tend to develop on the tip and shaft of the penis and on the scrotum, as well as in and around the anus.

> These genital warts may be small red or white bumps; tiny, cauliflower-like clusters; or flat, flesh-colored bumps that are barely visible.

The Obscure Epidemic

After the AIDS outbreak was first announced in the early 1980s, the public quickly became aware of HIV and its relationship to AIDS. News programs spotlighted it night after night; prolific articles and books were written about it; billboards warned about it; and physicians, hospitals, and public health agencies began to educate patients about it. Before long, people had become very cognizant of the virus and how dangerous it was, as well as how easily it could be spread from person to person. Today knowledge about HIV is widespread, and most everyone knows that it can lead to AIDS. Unfortunately, the same awareness does not exist about HPV.

Although its potential may not be as deadly as HIV, HPV infection is far more prevalent and infection rates are growing much faster. According to the CDC, about 56,000 people in the United States become infected with HIV each year, compared to *6 million* who are infected each year with HPV. Yet in spite of that, many people do not know much, if anything, about HPV—and surprisingly enough, that lack of awareness includes some health-care professionals. A national survey published in the December 2006 issue of the journal *Pediatrics* showed that although 98 percent of the physicians surveyed were aware that HPV caused genital warts in males and females, close to one-third were unaware that HPV was responsible for nearly all cases of cervical cancer. In addition, when asked whether HPV was a relatively uncommon sexually transmitted infection, 12.7 percent incorrectly answered that it was, and 3.8 percent did not know. Obviously, if physicians themselves are unclear about the risks posed by HPV, it is not difficult to see why awareness is so low among the general public.

In some cases physicians knew that women were infected with HPV but, for whatever reason, did not pass this information along. In 1988 when Kath Mazzella was 37 years old, her Pap test was abnormal, so she underwent laser treatment on her cervix. Six years later, believing that she was in good health, Mazzella was diagnosed with cervical cancer and had to undergo major gynecological surgery. Afterward she found out that her doctor had known she was infected with HPV at the time of the abnormal Pap in 1988—and had documented it in her medical records—without saying anything to her about it. She was angry that this crucial information had not been given to her, because her cancer might have been prevented. "This was when I first learned that HPV can be a risk factor for cancer," she writes. "It was only after my discovery that it was explained what HPV was. I felt completely betrayed that I had not been informed about the risk of this virus. I feel I was not informed correctly, yet today some nine years after I first learned about HPV I still hear that women are very much in the dark and confused. Many suffer in silence. . . . Something needs to be done."[20]

According to the CDC, about 56,000 people in the United States become infected with HIV each year, compared to *6 million* who are infected each year with HPV.

The "Tree Man"

One of the most bizarre cases of HPV infection was discovered in a remote village in the wilderness of Indonesia. A man named Dede Koswara had cut his knee in an accident when he was a teenager, and not long afterward a small wart developed on his lower leg. Over the next 20 years more warts developed, and they began to grow and spread uncontrollably. By the time Dede was 34 years old, enormous growths that resembled twisted tree roots were protruding from his hands and feet, and huge warts dominated his face and covered his body. He had formerly made his living as a fisherman, but the growths became so huge and unwieldy that Dede was no longer able to work, walk properly, or even use his hands. Local doctors were totally baffled by his condition and had no idea what to do to help him. Because of his grotesque appearance, Dede, who became known as the "Tree Man," was often the victim of abuse and ridicule by other villagers. He lived in fear that the growths would eventually cover his eyes and mouth, which would leave him unable to eat or breathe.

> " By the time Dede was 34 years old, enormous growths that resembled twisted tree roots were protruding from his hands and feet, and huge warts dominated his face and covered his body. "

In 2007 Anthony Gaspari, a renowned expert in skin conditions from the University of Maryland, became aware of Dede's mysterious condition and traveled to Indonesia to consult with him. He describes his initial reaction at meeting the man: "I've never seen anything like this in my entire career."[21] After taking samples of the growths from Dede's skin and testing them, Gaspari determined that they were caused by an extremely rare form of HPV. Dede apparently had a genetic condition that impeded his immune system so he had no ability to fight off the infection.

Gaspari began treating him with daily doses of a synthetic form of vitamin A to shrink the warts, and Dede also underwent a series of operations over a 6-month period. Surgeons were able to remove 95 percent of the growths—with a total weight of 13 pounds (6kg)—from his face, arms, and legs. In March 2008, for the first time in 20 years, Dede was able to walk without pain, and by August he had completed his ninth surgery and was released from the hospital. After years of being totally dependent on others to take care of him, Dede was able to not only walk but also hold a pen and write, eat by himself, use a cell phone, and do Sudoku puzzles. Although doctors have warned him that the warts may grow back, Dede's condition is no longer life threatening and his quality of life has improved immensely. In an interview with the news media he said he hoped to be able to find a job, and perhaps someday get married.

A Long Way to Go

A great deal has been learned about HPV since Shope discovered its contagious properties in the early 1930s by studying rabbits. Scientists have identified over 100 types of HPV and they know which areas of the body the viruses typically infect, as well as the symptoms they cause. They are also aware that in many cases no symptoms appear at all, so people have no idea that they are infected. Still, however, much is not known. Public awareness of HPV remains relatively low, and even many health-care professionals lack sufficient knowledge about HPV. Hopefully this will change in the near future—because if it does not, HPV will continue to spread at unprecedented rates and infect people throughout the world.

Primary Source Quotes*

What Is HPV?

❝Warts are noncancerous skin growths caused by the human papillomavirus (HPV). Many different types of HPV exist that can cause warts.❞

—Erica Monteiro, "Warts—Part I," Skin Type Solutions, September 1, 2008. http://skintypesolutions.com.

Monteiro is a cosmetic dermatologist at Federal University of Sao Paulo, Brazil.

❝Most Americans are probably more familiar with HIV than HPV, or human papilloma virus, although HPV affects millions more people.❞

—Donnica Moore, "What Is HPV?" DrDonnica.com, August 29, 2005. www.drdonnica.com.

Moore is a women's health expert, physician educator, and media commentator.

* Editor's Note: While the definition of a primary source can be narrowly or broadly defined, for the purposes of Compact Research, a primary source consists of: 1) results of original research presented by an organization or researcher; 2) eyewitness accounts of events, personal experience, or work experience; 3) first-person editorials offering pundits' opinions; 4) government officials presenting political plans and/or policies; 5) representatives of organizations presenting testimony or policy.

"Genital HPV is the most common sexually transmitted infection in the United States, with approximately 6.2 million people becoming newly infected each year."

—Douglas Holt, "HPV Vaccine: A Little Pain Now, Cancer Protection Later," ABC News, January 7, 2008. http://hscweb3.hsc.usf.edu.

Holt is a professor in the Division of Infectious Disease and International Medicine at the University of South Florida College of Medicine.

"There are more than 100 types of HPV, some of which cause common warts found on areas like hands and feet."

—Joanne Poje Tomasulo and David Lubetkin, "HPV & Women," review, NBC/iVillage Your Total Health, June 13, 2007. http://yourtotalhealth.ivillage.com.

Tomasulo is a physician in Ironton, Ohio; and Lubetkin is a physician in Boca Raton, Florida.

"An estimated 75 percent of sexually active adults have or will have transmitted human papillomavirus (HPV) at some point in their lifetimes."

—Joel Palefsky, "HPV 101: What Your Doctor May Not Tell You About HPV and Abnormal Pap Smears," Not Alone, 2002. www.enotalone.com.

Palefsky is a professor at the University of California at San Francisco and a leading HPV expert.

❝ Think of it like this—virtually everybody who has sex is exposed to HPV, but the vast majority of HPV infections just flush out of a woman's body. ❞

—Sanjay Gupta, "New Test for HPV," CNN Paging Dr. Gupta Blog, October 18, 2007. www.cnn.com.

Gupta is a practicing neurosurgeon and chief medical correspondent for the health and medical unit at CNN.

❝ There has been no satisfactory explanation as to why warts develop in some people but never in others. ❞

—Edward Villablança, "The HPV Organism and the Different Types of Warts It Causes," Associated Content, August 30, 2007. www.associatedcontent.com.

Villablanca is a biotechnologist from Suisan City, California.

❝ Infection with HPV is common, with as many as 20 million persons infected in the United States alone. Worldwide, there are more than 440 million individuals with HPV infection. ❞

—Janet M. Torpy, "Human Papillomavirus Infection," *Journal of the American Medical Association*, February 28, 2007, p. 912.

Torpy is a physician and medical writer.

66 Because HPVs are difficult to grow in cell culture or animal models, less is known about them than other pathogens of equal importance. **99**

—Rebecca J. Greenblatt, "Human Papillomaviruses: Diseases, Diagnosis, and a Possible Vaccine," *Clinical Microbiology Newsletter,* September 2005. www.sciencedirect.com.

Greenblatt is with the Department of Microbiology and Immunology at SUNY Upstate Medical University in Syracuse, New York.

66 While many people think HPV is mostly a problem for teens or young adults, HPV virus can infect men and women of any age. **99**

—Brunilda Nazario, "HPV Virus: Information About Human Papillomavirus," WebMD, April 18, 2007. www.webmd.com.

Nazario is a physician who is responsible for reviewing WebMD news, feature stories, and graphics.

66 Overall in the United States, an estimated 6.2 million new HPV infections occur every year among persons aged 14–44 years. Of these, 74% occur among those aged 15–24 years. **99**

—Lauri E. Markowitz et al., "Quadrivalent Human Papillomavirus Vaccine," *CDC Morbidity and Morbidity Weekly Report,* March 23, 2007. www.cdc.gov.

Markowitz is a physician who works for the CDC in Atlanta.

What Is HPV?

- HPV is not a single virus but rather a group of more than **100 related viruses**, each of which has been assigned a number.

- HPV is the most common sexually transmitted disease, with more than **6 million new infections** in the United States each year.

- The American Medical Association (AMA) reports that more than **440 million** people worldwide are infected with HPV, including an estimated **20 million** in the United States.

- An estimated **50 percent** of all HPV infections reported in the United States occur in people between the ages of 15 and 25.

- One study of 3,000 women by the National Cancer Institute revealed that only **40 percent** of them had ever heard of HPV.

- A study published in the *Journal of the American Medical Association* showed that among women in the United States, **45 percent** of those aged 14 to 19 tested positive for one or more types of HPV in 2007, compared to **19 percent** of women aged 50 to 59 who were infected.

- The Mayo Clinic states that each type of HPV has the potential to cause **abnormal growths** on a particular part of the body.

Wart-Causing Viruses

HPV comprises a group of more than 100 related viruses. It can cause many types of warts on different areas of the body. These warts can develop on cutaneous skin, which is the visible skin that covers the entire body, and mucosal membranes, which are warm, skin-like layers that line the inside of the mouth, as well as the vagina, anus, head of the penis, and other body cavities that open to the outside. This chart shows some of the most common warts, where they typically appear on the body, and the HPV types that cause them.

Cutaneous or Mucosal Disorder	Location	HPV Types
Common warts	Mostly hands	1, 2, 4, 26, 27, 41, 57, 65
Plantar warts	Bottom of feet	1, 2, 4, 63
Mosaic warts	Hands, feet	2, 27, 57
Flat warts	Arms, face, knees	3, 10, 27, 28, 38, 41, 49
Butcher's warts (common in people who handle meat, poultry, and fish)	Hands	1, 2, 3, 4, 7, 10, 28
Laryngeal papilloma	Larynx, upper respiratory tract	6, 11, 30
Oral leukoplakia	Mucous membranes of the cheek, gums, or tongue	16, 18
Conjunctival papilloma	Eyelid	6, 11
Maxillary sinus papilloma	Sinus cavities	57
Epidermodysplasia verruciformis (chronic wart-like lesions)	Any cutaneous skin exposed to light	5, 8, 9, 12, 14, 15, 17, 19, 20, 21, 22, 23, 24, 25, 36, 47, 50
Genital warts	Women: the vulva, around the clitoris, in an around the anus, and on the linings of the vagina, cervix, and rectum Men: the tip and shaft of the penis, on the scrotum, in and around the anus	6, 11, 30, 42, 43, 44, 45, 51, 52, 54

Sources: Peter A. Gearhart, "Human Papillomavirus," eMedicine, January 19, 2007. www.emedicine.com; John D. Shanley, "Papillomavirus," eMedicine, August 15, 2007. www.emedicine.com.

- HPVs can cause common and **plantar warts**, most often on the hands, fingers, toes, and feet; other HPV strains can cause warts in the genital areas of males and females.

- The CDC states that about **1 percent** of sexually active adults in the United States have genital warts at any one time.

The Most Common Sexually Transmitted Infections

A study released in March 2008 by the Centers for Disease Control and Prevention (CDC) analyzed data from 838 females from ages 14 to 19, and found that 26 percent had at least one sexually transmitted infection (STI). This graph shows which STIs were the most common among participants.

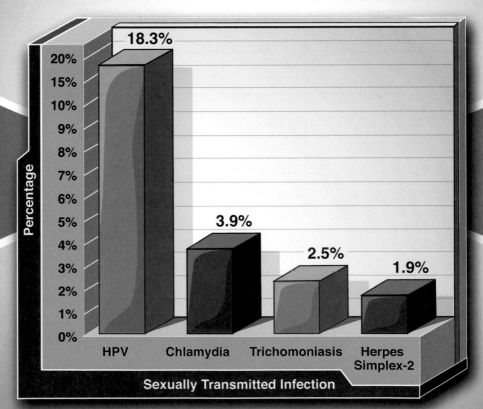

Source: Centers for Disease Control and Prevention (CDC), "2008 National STD Prevention Conference," March 11, 2008. www.cdc.gov.

Who Gets HPVs?

A study published in the February 28, 2007, issue of the *Journal of the American Medical Association* examined the prevalence of low- and high-risk types of HPV in females ages 14 to 59. This graph shows which age groups were most likely to be infected with the various types.

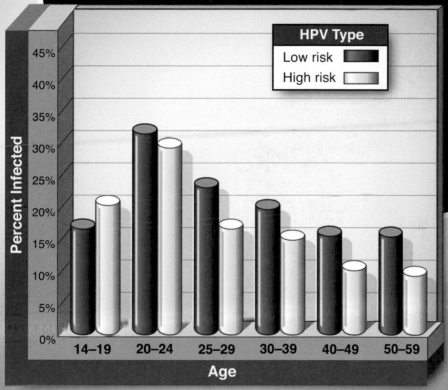

Note: Low-risk HPV types include 6, 11, 32, 40, 42, 44, 54, 55, 61, 62, 64, 71, 72, 74, 81, 83, 84, 87, 89, and 91. High-risk HPV types include 16, 18, 26, 31, 33, 35, 39, 45, 51, 52, 53, 56, 58, 59, 66, 67, 68, 69, 70, 73, 82, 85, and IS39. Both low-risk and high-risk HPV types were detected in some females.

Source: Eileen F. Dunne et al., "Prevalence of HPV Infection Among Females in the United States," *Journal of the American Medical Association*, February 28, 2007. http://jama.ama-assn.org.

- HPV types 6 and 11 cause about **90 percent** of all genital warts.

- According to the November 2005 issue of *AIDS Treatment Update*, **gay and bisexual men** are twice as likely as heterosexuals to be diagnosed with genital warts.

Public Awareness of HPVs

According to a November 2006 study by the National Cancer Institute, many women in the United States are uniformed about HPV, and a majority of them have never even heard of it. These charts show how the participants responded to various questions.

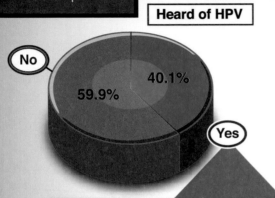

Heard of HPV

No
59.9%
40.1%
Yes

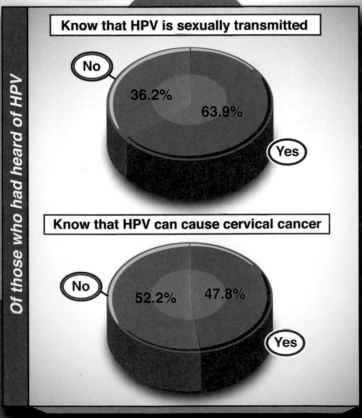

Of those who had heard of HPV

Know that HPV is sexually transmitted

No
36.2%
63.9%
Yes

Know that HPV can cause cervical cancer

No
52.2%
47.8%
Yes

Source: Jasmin A. Tiro et al., "What Do Women in the U.S. Know About Human Papillomavirus and Cervical Cancer?" *Cancer Epidemiology Biomarkers & Prevention*, February 2007. http://cebp.aacrjournals.org.

What Causes HPV Infection?

> ❝ HPV infection occurs when the virus enters your body through a cut, abrasion or imperceptible tear in the outer layer of your skin. . . . HPV infections associated with genital warts and related lesions are contracted through sexual intercourse, anal sex and other skin-to-skin contact in the genital regions. ❞
>
> —Mayo Clinic, "HPV Infection."

> ❝ In virtually all studies of HPV prevalence and incidence, the most consistent predictors of infection have been measures of sexual activity, most importantly the number of sex partners (lifetime and recent). ❞
>
> —Lauri E. Markowitz et al., *CDC Morbidity and Morbidity Weekly Report.*

Even with the vast amount of knowledge that scientists have gained throughout the years, when and how HPVs and other viruses originated remains a mystery. These organisms are widely believed to be remnants of the ancient past, but they still present far more questions than answers. Ed Rybicki, a virologist from Cape Town, South Africa, explains:

> Tracing the origins of viruses is difficult because they don't leave fossils and because of the tricks they use to make copies of themselves within the cells they've invaded. Some viruses even have the ability to stitch their own genes into those of the cells they infect, which means studying their ancestry requires untangling it from the history of their

hosts and other organisms. What makes the process even more complicated is that viruses don't just infect humans; they can infect basically any organism—from bacteria to horses; seaweed to people.[22]

Rybicki's reference to "infect" is important because scientists know that viruses are responsible for a wide variety of infections, ranging from the common cold to influenza and other deadly diseases—and unlike bacterial infections, those caused by viruses cannot be treated or cured with antibiotics. HPVs, like all viruses, can and do cause infections. Some of the viruses are relatively harmless, while others are much more dangerous and can be life threatening.

HPV Types and Infection

It has long been known that HPVs infect the skin rather than the blood, bones, or internal organs such as the brain, liver, and heart. HPV expert Joel Palefsky refers to skin as a person's "coat of armor," saying that it "protects us from the environment and keeps us healthy."[23] Humans have two types of skin: cutaneous, which is the visible skin that covers the body from the top of the head down to the toes; and mucosal, which refers to the mucous membranes, the warm, skin-like layers that line the inside of the mouth as well as the vagina, anus, head of the penis, and other cavities that open to the outside of the body. These areas are kept moist by mucus that is excreted from the glands, which creates an ideal environment for HPVs to flourish.

> "HPVs, like all viruses, can and do cause infections. Some of the viruses are relatively harmless, while others are much more dangerous and can be life threatening."

HPVs that infect cutaneous skin enter the body through cuts, scratches, or microscopic tears in the outer layer of the skin. Such viruses thrive in warm, moist environments and may be transmitted from one person to another through skin-to-skin contact as well as through shared towels, locker-room floors, public showers and bathhouses, and swimming pool platforms, among other sources. Although many people exposed to HPVs do not become infected, those who do may develop warts on various parts of the body such as the hands, fingers, feet, toes, and face. These warts—which are usually caused by common, low-risk HPV types 1, 2, 4, and 7—cannot only be spread from person to person but also from one part of an infected individual's body to another part, such as from the toes to the fingers or face. The HPV types that cause common, plantar, or other types of warts on cutaneous skin do not favor the mucosal skin of the genital tract, so these HPVs are not believed to be linked to genital warts. Palefsky explains: "Remember— the genital HPV types live only in the genital skin, and not in the other parts of your skin, such as your hands, face, and so on. So you can't get a genital HPV infection by touching the hand or foot of someone with warts in those places."[24]

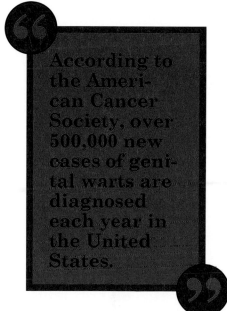

According to the American Cancer Society, over 500,000 new cases of genital warts are diagnosed each year in the United States.

The HPVs that infect mucosal membranes *do* prefer the genital areas, and that is where the viruses thrive. Although men can and do become infected with genital HPVs, women tend to develop the infection more often. Health-care professionals believe this is because the vagina is lined with warm, moist mucous membranes that are easy for viruses to pass through, and this makes for a very hospitable environment for viral growth. The most common low-risk HPVs that typically infect the genitalia are types 6 and 11, which are highly contagious and can lead to the formation of genital warts in men and women. These warts are extremely common in people who have been infected by a genital HPV. According to the American Cancer Society, over 500,000 new cases of genital warts are diagnosed each year in the United States. They are the only visible sign of HPV infection, but the warts may not appear for weeks, months, or even years after someone has been infected. In many cases they do not appear at all. In fact, most people who are infected with HPV never develop warts; but because the virus lives under the skin, even without any visible symptoms HPV can still be transmitted from one person to another. Oregon physician Kathy Greaves says that, "recent research shows that MOST cases of transmission occur during asymptomatic periods, or times when the infected person has no visible warts."[25]

Because HPV infection often remains hidden, and genital HPVs are so highly contagious, people may unknowingly pass HPV along to those with whom they are sexually intimate. This occurs as a result of genital-to-genital contact, whereby the viruses spread when an infected person's genitalia rubs against another person's genitalia. Although this happens most commonly through vaginal or anal intercourse, HPVs may be spread in other ways as well. Steven L. Harris, director of the Student Health Center at San Jose State University, explains: "You can just sleep naked with somebody, being in skin-to-skin contact, and get (certain infections)."[26] However, reports of HPV infection that involved oral-to-genital or hand-to-genital sex play, including the sharing of sex toys, are much rarer. Julie Gerberding, director of the CDC, cites a study of college-aged women in Seattle that showed a 2-year genital HPV incidence rate of 39 percent among sexually active women, compared to an 8 percent infection rate among women who had not engaged in intercourse.

The Risk of Multiple Partners

It is common knowledge among scientists and medical professionals that even if a person has sex only one time, he or she is at risk for contracting a genital HPV infection. The fact remains, however, that the more sexual partners one has, the greater the risk for being infected with HPV. The same is true for someone whose partner has been involved in multiple sexual relationships. According to Gerberding, the Seattle study of college students found that young women whose male sex partners had at least one prior partner had a fivefold risk of developing HPV infection compared to those whose male partners had not previously had sexual relations. The same study showed that women whose male partners had an unknown number of prior sexual relations had an eightfold risk of acquiring HPV infection. Gerberding describes another finding: "This study also reported that women who had known a sex partner at least eight months before initiating a sexual relationship were less likely to acquire genital HPV infection. It was hypothesized that this was due to a greater chance of spontaneous clearance of infection in men who might have been infected with HPV in a previous sexual relationship."[27]

A young woman who posted anonymously to an HPV Web forum spoke candidly about her experience of being intimate with someone who had previously been with multiple partners. When she was 16 years old, she vowed to remain a virgin, and even withheld her first kiss, until she found a partner who was very special to her, someone she considered to be "the one." Then she met a boy named Eric, and thinking that she had found her true love, she became sexually involved with him. Several months passed, during which they continued to have sex and always used a condom. She began to find the experience unfulfilling and agreed to continue seeing Eric only if they refrained from sex. They broke up not long afterward, and after dating several other boys she became involved with Marc. One night "in the heat of the moment" they had sex without using a condom, but she was not too concerned, as she explains: "I knew that he had a history of being with a lot of girls, sometimes without using protection. It's funny how quickly you can push a worry like that aside when caught up in a 'moment.'"[28]

> " It is common knowledge among scientists and medical professionals that even if a person has sex only one time, he or she is at risk for contracting a genital HPV infection. "

Two months later, after her doctor phoned to say that her Pap test had come back abnormal, she received the news that she was HPV-positive. Further tests showed that she had been infected with a high-risk HPV type and had cancerous cells on her cervix, which she later had removed with minor surgery. She is now hopefully cancer free, but she realizes that the virus will always be inside her body. "Now my life is forever changed," she writes.

> I'll never get used to waking up every day and realizing that my odds of getting cervical cancer are permanently hiked. The best advice I can give to teens is to be abstinent. But I understand how unrealistic that is for many. So, the next best thing is to truly know whom you're having sex with. Talk to each other. Know your partner's sexual history. If

your partner has been with a lot of people, you'd better make sure he or she has been tested for STDs. . . . I can't turn back time. And now, because of a moment's desire, I suffer from a lifelong STD. But you don't have to. Take care of yourselves—now and always.[29]

The Risk for Babies

When people hear about HPVs, they typically think of sexually transmitted viruses because genital HPVs are highly contagious and infections are so common. But HPVs can be passed along in other ways as well, and in some cases may even infect newborn babies. As Georgetown University Medical Center's Richard Schlegel writes: "Although sex is the most common mechanism for transmitting the virus, it is not the only way. For example, during birth, babies can be infected in their airway by passing through the birth canal of an infected mother."[30] If a newborn is infected with HPV, this may result in a rare condition called recurrent respiratory papillomatosis, which causes the development of wart-like tumors in the throat, usually on the larynx or on and around the vocal cords. These growths can be surgically removed, although they have a tendency to grow back (hence, the term "recurrent").

> Research that was announced in July 2008 showed that newborns could possibly contract HPV in another way—by drinking the mother's breast milk.

Research that was announced in July 2008 showed that newborns could possibly contract HPV in another way—by drinking the mother's breast milk. In a study led by oral pathologist Stina Syrjänen, a team of researchers from a university in Turku, Finland, obtained cervical and oral scrapings from 223 mothers, and oral scrapings from 87 fathers. The detection rate of high-risk HPV was 12 to 15 percent in samples from the mothers' cervixes and 20 to 24 percent in their oral samples; the high-risk HPV detection rate in the fathers' oral samples was higher, from 21 to 26 percent. After the babies were born, HPV was detected in 10 (4.5 percent) of the breast milk samples that were collected, and the researchers confirmed that the virus was high-risk HPV type 16. They theorized that the HPV's presence in the breast milk could have been passed from either the mother or the father. After the completion of the research, Syrjänen stated that if HPV particles are able to survive in breast milk, it is possible for an infant to be infected with HPV during breast-feeding.

The Uncertainty Lingers

Like all viruses, HPVs are infectious organisms that can be transmitted from one person to another. They comprise a number of forms, from the HPV types that linger on locker-room floors and cause common warts to the more highly contagious HPVs that thrive in mucosal areas and result in genital warts. In many cases, transmission of genital HPV infection occurs without carriers having any symptoms, which means they do not know that they have been infected and have no way of knowing that they are putting their partners at risk. Because no virus, including any of the HPV types, can be cured with antibiotics or other medications, once someone has been infected the virus lives in his or her body forever. Over time a person's immune system is likely to fight the virus off and cause it to become dormant, but no one can know that for sure; as a result, the possibility remains that the infection can be passed along to someone else. Scientists can only hope that research will eventually lead to a cure for HPV. If it does, then the epidemic that now seems to be unstoppable may someday become a thing of the past.

What Causes HPV Infection?

❝Warts are caused by a human virus, not by kissing (or even holding) a frog. The specific virus that causes warts is the human papilloma virus (HPV), of which there are at least 60 types.❞

—Mitchell Hecht, "Ask Dr. H: The Causes and the Cures for Warts," *Philadelphia Inquirer,* June 30, 2008. www.philly.com.

Hecht is a physician who specializes in internal medicine.

❝It horrifies me to think that women may be undergoing hysterectomies, cancer cell removal, vulvectomies and also dying, without being aware of the link with HPV.❞

—Kath Mazzella, "Kath's Story—A Personal Experience with HPV," *Australian Health Consumer,* 2003–2004. www.chf.org.

Mazzella is a survivor of cervical cancer who founded the Gynaecological Awareness Information Network (GAIN).

* Editor's Note: While the definition of a primary source can be narrowly or broadly defined, for the purposes of Compact Research, a primary source consists of: 1) results of original research presented by an organization or researcher; 2) eyewitness accounts of events, personal experience, or work experience; 3) first-person editorials offering pundits' opinions; 4) government officials presenting political plans and/or policies; 5) representatives of organizations presenting testimony or policy.

66 Genital HPV is transmitted mainly by direct genital contact during vaginal or anal intercourse. It is not spread through bodily fluids, nor does it live in blood, or any organs. 99

—American Cancer Society, "Frequently Asked Questions About Human Papilloma Virus (HPV) Vaccines," December 4, 2007. www.cancer.org.

The American Cancer Society is a leading cancer research organization whose mission is to prevent cancer, save lives, and diminish suffering from cancer.

66 The [HPV] virus is passed on very easily. It's important to remember the wart virus is most often spread during intimate contact, when infected skin rubs against uninfected skin, rather than being spread by semen, vaginal secretions or blood. 99

—Trisha Macnair, "Human Papilloma Virus (HPV)," BBC Health, May 2008. www.bbc.co.uk.

Macnair is a physician, medical journalist, and broadcaster in the United Kingdom.

66 HPV infections that do not go away can 'hide' in the body for years and not be detected. That's why it is impossible to know exactly when someone got infected, how long they've been infected, or who passed the infection to them. 99

—Planned Parenthood, "HPV," February 21, 2008. www.plannedparenthood.org.

Planned Parenthood is a leading women's health-care provider, educator, and advocate.

66 HPV is so common and transmissible that having just one sexual partner often results in infection. Indeed, cumulative prevalence rates are as high as 82% among adolescent women in select populations. 99

—Anna-Barbara Moscicki, "Impact of HPV Infection in Adolescent Populations,"
Journal of Adolescent Health, December 2005. www.ncbi.nlm.nih.gov.

Moscicki is a professor of pediatrics at the University of California–San Francisco Medical School's Division of Adolescent Medicine.

66 Visible genital warts appear only during active infection. But it is possible to spread the virus even if you can't see the warts. 99

—Robin Parks, "Genital Warts (Human Papillovirus)," Kaiser Permanente Health Encyclopedia, August 17, 2006.

Parks writes for Kaiser Permanente, a managed health-care organization based in Oakland, California.

66 Not having sex is the surest way to prevent HPV infections. Reducing the number of sexual partners and using condoms will reduce the risk of getting an HPV infection, but may not entirely prevent infection. 99

—Minnesota Department of Health (MDH), "Human Papillomavirus:
What You Should Know," February 2008. www.health.state.mn.us.

The MDH is dedicated to protecting, maintaining, and improving the health of people who live in Minnesota.

66 HPV is transmitted through vaginal, anal, and oral sex and can be transmitted by skin-to-skin genital contact or rubbing. HPV can spread whether or not warts are visible. 99

—Brown University Health Services, "Human Papilloma Virus (Genital Warts)," September 5, 2008. www.brown.edu.

Brown University Health Services facilitates workshops, offers individual counseling and referrals, and coordinates special events on a wide range of health-related topics.

66 Genital ulcer diseases and HPV infections can occur in both male or female genital areas that are covered or protected by a latex condom, as well as in areas that are not covered. 99

—Barbara K. Hecht and Frederick Hecht, "Condoms and Sexually Transmitted Diseases (STDs)," eMedicine Health, May 24, 2007. www.emedicinehealth.com.

Barbara Hecht is director of Hecht Associates, consultants in medical genetics, in Jacksonville, Florida; and Frederick Hecht is a pediatrician and medical geneticist in Scottsdale, Arizona.

66 Because HPV is so common, it is difficult to avoid it altogether. It is reasonable to expect that you will get HPV at some time during your life. Sexual contact with just one partner can be enough to get or spread the virus. 99

—QIAGEN, "What Men Need to Know About HPV," 2006. www.thehpvtest.com.

QIAGEN is a technology development organization that is committed to advancing women's health.

What Causes HPV Infection?

- HPV infection occurs when viral particles find their way into the human body, **invade cells**, and reproduce, which eventually destroys the "host" cells and releases more viral material.

- It is a myth that people catch warts from **toads** or any other animals.

- HPVs that infect **cutaneous skin** enter the body through cuts, scratches, or imperceptible tears in the outer layer of the skin.

- HPVs that infect **mucosal membranes** are most commonly spread through sexual intercourse (anal or vaginal), skin-to-skin contact, or oral sex.

- Condoms may help protect against genital HPV, but because some infected areas remain uncovered they **do not provide 100 percent** protection.

- The HPVs that cause common warts are not the same types that cause **genital warts**.

- An estimated **90 percent** of people who are infected with HPV develop no visible symptoms, which means they can spread the infection without being aware that they even have it.

How Viruses Infect the Body

Viruses, which enter the body through breaks, scratches, or imperceptible tears in the skin, are microscopic fragments of nucleic acid that are enclosed in protein shells. Unlike cells and bacteria, HPVs and other viruses cannot reproduce on their own; instead, they must invade living "host" cells and use the cells as factories where they produce more viral material, and in this way they lead to various types of infection. This illustration shows the progression.

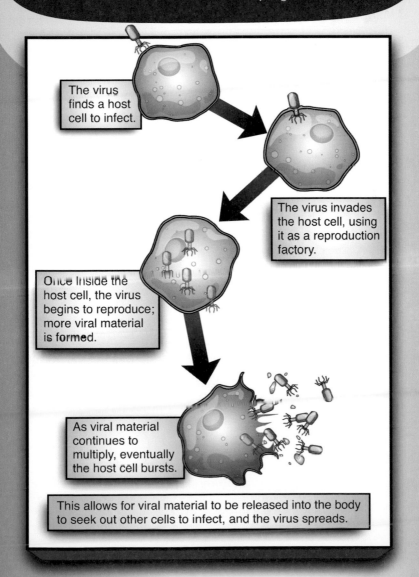

The virus finds a host cell to infect.

The virus invades the host cell, using it as a reproduction factory.

Once inside the host cell, the virus begins to reproduce; more viral material is formed.

As viral material continues to multiply, eventually the host cell bursts.

This allows for viral material to be released into the body to seek out other cells to infect, and the virus spreads.

Source: Craig Freudenrich, "How Viruses Work," How Stuff Works, 2000. http://health.howstuffworks.com.

- Although it is rare, **mothers** with genital warts may infect their **newborn babies** delivered through vaginal delivery; this may lead to HPV infection in the baby's genitals or upper respiratory system.

- **Towels, locker-room floors, shared showers, and swimming pool** platforms are areas where wart-causing HPVs (not genital) are commonly transmitted from one person to another.

- Someone can become infected with HPV after just **one sexual encounter**, although those with multiple partners have a much higher risk of developing infection.

Risk Factors for Genital HPV Infection

Genital HPVs are highly contagious viruses that can be contracted in a variety of ways. Although having just one sexual encounter can lead to HPV infection, a number of lifestyle factors can increase the risk, as this table shows.

Risk Factors
Becoming sexually active at a young age
Having numerous sexual partners
Having sex with someone who has had numerous sexual partners
Having unprotected sex (no condom use)
Engaging in oral sex with five or more partners
Cigarette smoking
Excessive alcohol consumption
Being infected with the human immunodeficiency virus (HIV)
Having a weak or impaired immune system

Sources: American Cancer Society, "Frequently Asked Questions About Human Papilloma Virus (HPV) Vaccines," July 20, 2008. www.cancer.org; Mayo Clinic, "HPV Infection," March 13, 2007. www.mayoclinic.com.

How HPVs Are Spread

People who become infected with HPVs contract the viruses in a number of ways, and they often do not develop any symptoms. If symptoms do develop, the immune system fights off the viruses in as many as 90 percent of cases. This table shows how HPVs are commonly spread and the typical signs of infection.

Activity That Can Spread HPV Infection	Possibly Leads to . . .
Sharing towels, walking barefoot in public showers and/or bathhouses, walking on swimming pool platforms	Common, plantar, flat, and other non-malignant warts on the feet, hands, and face
Vaginal sex	Genital warts, premalignant genital lesions, cellular abnormalities
Anal sex	Genital warts, premalignant genital lesions, cellular abnormalities
Oral sex	Warts on the tongue, gums, tonsils, soft palate, larynx, nose, throat
Oral-gential and hand-genital sex play, sharing of sex toys	Genital warts, premalignant genital lesions, cellular abnormalities
Any skin-to-skin genital contact	Genital warts, premalignant genital lesions, cellular abnormalities
Vaginal delivery of newborn by mother who has genital warts as the result of HPV infection	Warts on the baby's genitals or in the throat or respiratory tract (very rare)

Sources: American Cancer Society, "Frequently Asked Questions About Human Papilloma Virus (HPV) Vaccines," July 20, 2008. www.cancer.org; Mayo Clinic, "HPV Infection," March 15, 2007. www.mayoclinic.com.

What Are the Health Risks of Genital HPV Infection?

>**❝**With cancer of the uterine cervix, HPV is responsible for nearly 100% of the cancers, and this is true for all parts of the world. That's very surprising, very unusual. It's the only example of a major human cancer that has a single etiology.**❞**
>
> —Keerti Shah, "Human Papillomavirus."

>**❝**Once you hear that your cancer is linked to HPV, you review every item in the file, looking for the moment you made the Wrong Choice. But it's impossible. It's not one interaction; it's my entire life's web of meeting people, everything that took me to various experiences and relationships.**❞**
>
> —Stephen Reynolds, *Reader's Digest.*

During the 1960s researchers were beginning to seriously explore the connection between viruses and various types of cancer. In a case report published in 1963, Canadian pathologist Elizabeth Stern was the first to show that a definite causative relationship existed, and she was convinced that cervical cancer was caused by the herpes simplex virus. Although this connection was later proven to be erroneous, it continued to be the prevailing scientific belief throughout the 1960s and most of the 1970s.

German virologist Harald zur Hausen was pursuing his own research on viruses and their relationship to cancer during this same period of time. Although he was aware that cervical cancer was the result of a sexually transmitted virus, he was highly skeptical about the claims that it was caused by herpes simplex. Instead, he was convinced that the real culprit was the human papillomavirus. Working with his colleagues at the University of Erlangen-Nuremberg in Bavaria, zur Hausen discovered a number of different human papillomaviruses. As he continued to pursue his research, he became even more convinced that scientific beliefs about the connection between the herpes simplex virus and cervical cancer were flawed. In 1974 zur Hausen traveled to Florida to present his research findings at an international virology conference—findings that were controversial because they refuted years of accepted scientific theories. His message was not at all well received by the other scientists, as Peter McIntyre writes: "The audience listened to zur Hausen in stony silence, and dismissed his (now vindicated) results as lacking sensitivity. It was the low point of his professional life."[31]

A Lifesaving Test

In August 2004 Frances Masterman attended a networking breakfast in Chesterton, Indiana, where she heard a presentation by an obstetrician/gynecologist and one by a survivor of cervical cancer. Both speakers strongly urged the women in attendance to be regularly tested for HPV, in addition to having regular Pap tests. Prior to that, Masterman had never even heard of HPV, so she had no idea that it was the leading cause of cervical cancer. She took the women's advice, and at her next gynecological checkup she requested an HPV test. Her nurse practitioner said that such a test was unnecessary unless her Pap showed abnormal results, but Masterman insisted. She explains: "She protested, saying they'd have to charge extra, and like a broken record, I kept telling her, 'I want the test,' until she finally ordered it." When the results came back, the physician and nurse practitioner were both shocked. "I had, in

> As he continued to pursue his research, [zur Hausen] became even more convinced that scientific beliefs about the connection between the herpes simplex virus and cervical cancer were flawed.

fact, tested positive for HPV and my Pap test had failed to identify my increased risk," Masterman writes. "Now I am being monitored more closely to make sure any cervical changes are caught before they become cancerous. You'd better believe I ask questions when I'm at the doctor's office now. Demanding that HPV test just might have saved my life."[32]

Like Masterman, many women are not aware of the dangers posed by HPV, nor do they know about its connection to cervical cancer. And even if they do have this awareness, women are often not aware that Pap tests are not as accurate as tests that are specifically designed to detect HPVs. In a study of more than 10,000 women ages 30 to 69, which was published in October 2007 in the *New England Journal of Medicine*, researchers found that HPV tests detected 95 percent of cases in which participants had precancerous changes in the cervix, compared with 55 percent for the Pap test.

HPV and Cervical Cancer

Although cancers of the lungs and breast are the top 2 cancer-related killers of women each year, neither is caused by a virus as is cervical cancer. According to the American Cancer Society, nearly 100 percent of cervical cancers are the result of high-risk HPV infection. In the United States an estimated 10,000 women are diagnosed annually with cervical cancer, and nearly 4,000 die of the disease each year.

" Although cancers of the lungs and breast are the top two cancer-related killers of women each year, neither is caused by a virus as is cervical cancer. "

One woman who had a close brush with death from cervical cancer is Yvonne Gatens, whose annual Pap tests routinely came back normal. After her daughter was born in 1992, Gatens went to the doctor for her postnatal checkup—and she was totally unprepared to hear that not only did she have cervical cancer, the disease had progressed to the advanced stages. She was told that the HPV virus had apparently been lying dormant in her body for years, and it would likely have gone undetected if it had not been for her postpregnancy exam. "If I hadn't been pregnant,

I probably wouldn't have known there was anything wrong," she says. "If it had gone unnoticed, God knows what could have happened."[33] Gatens underwent surgery to remove the cancer and spent 10 days in the hospital. In 1997 she was given the welcome news that she was cancer free.

Liz Ellwood, another cervical cancer survivor, was diagnosed at age 24. Like many women, she was shocked to find out that her cancer was caused by HPV infection. Ellwood had a low risk for contracting a sexually transmitted disease (STD); she had become sexually active somewhat later in life, she had had few partners, all of her partners had been tested for STDs, and she had always used condoms for protection. By the time her Pap test came back abnormal, she was in the throes of clear cell adenocarcinoma, a rare type of cervical cancer that is often quite advanced by the time it is diagnosed and can be difficult for doctors to tell how far it has spread. Ellwood's fight with cancer was challenging and difficult. She went through surgery, radiation, and chemotherapy, and suffered from nausea, chronic fatigue, and premature hot flashes.

> " She was told that the HPV virus had apparently been lying dormant in her body for years, and it would likely have gone undetected if it had not been for her post-pregnancy exam. "

She says that cervical cancer is a "huge loss for a woman," as she explains: "It's a big battle to go through and if it can be prevented it should. I want to help prevent other girls from having to go through what I went through." She adds that women need to do their own research on HPV and cervical cancer, be well informed, and not hesitate to talk to their physicians—and never forget that any sexually active woman could be at risk. "You never know," she says. "If it happened to me it could happen to anyone."[34]

Males at Risk

Most HPV-related publicity focuses on the risk of cervical cancer, which is a major health problem for women in the United States and many other countries throughout the world. But recent studies have shown that other types of cancer are on the rise, some of which have been connected with HPVs that affect men as well as women. For instance, anal and penile cancer have been increasingly connected with high-risk HPVs, as have oral cancers. According to research published in the May 10, 2007, issue of the *New England Journal of Medicine*, HPV-related oral cancer rose steadily in men from 1973 to 2004, and HPVs now cause nearly as many cancers of the upper throat as tobacco and alcohol. The study involved taking blood and saliva samples from the throats of 100 patients who were diagnosed with cancers of the tonsils or back of the throat, as well as taking oral samples from 200 healthy people for comparison purposes. The researchers concluded that participants who had more than 5 oral-sex partners in their lifetimes were 250 percent more likely to have throat cancer than those who did not have oral sex. In the case of subjects whose malignant throat tumors tested positive for HPV type 16, those who had more than 5 oral-sex partners had a 750 percent increased risk of cancers caused by the HPV strain.

At the conclusion of the study, Maura Gillison, one of the Johns Hopkins researchers who took part in the research, explained the significance of the findings: "When you look at the cancers associated with HPV in men—including penile cancer, anal squamous cell carcinoma, oral cancers—it's very close to the number of cases of cervical cancer that occur in the U.S. in women every year. We need to adjust the public's perception . . . that only women are at risk."[35]

One Man's Struggle

Because of his healthy lifestyle, Stephen Reynolds, who lives in New York City, never even dreamed that he would develop throat cancer. In August 2006 he, his wife, and their young son were vacationing in Cape Cod. Reynolds had suffered from a sore throat for several weeks, and he found it painful to swallow, so when he returned to New York he visited an ear, nose, and throat surgeon. He was given antibiotics and steroid treatments, but they did not help, and his throat continued to get worse. Finally he had a biopsy and was completely taken aback by the results. Reynolds had a cancerous tumor at the base of his tongue, and he was told that this particular form of cancer was aggressive and the tumor was growing rapidly, necessitating the need for surgery as soon as possible. He shares the thoughts that went through his mind at the time:

All the while, I'm thinking, What did I do? What did I do? Everybody starts with that, I suppose, because the diagnosis seems so unlikely. I never smoked. As one of my oncologists told me . . . 'This used to be a VA hospital kind of thing, you know.' Smoke a pack a day for 30 years, wash it down with a pint of vodka—that's how you get throat cancer, and maybe lung cancer too. But here I am, a 45-year-old male with a graduate degree, a business strategist in the technology industry. Someone with my profile, a nonsmoker under 50, rarely got this disease.[36]

In discussions with his doctor, Reynolds learned that his cancer was caused by HPV, which he had no idea could infect men as well as women. He also learned that he had likely been infected through oral sex a number of years before. "Without a singular mistake to obsess over and regret," he writes, "I settle for parched fear and guilt. They say that the risk of contracting this cancer can be hundreds of times higher in people who've had more than five oral sex partners in their lifetime. How many times had I been exposed? How many times had I exposed others?"[37] The following months were physically painful and emotionally traumatic for Reynolds. After surgery he went through radiation and chemotherapy, which made him so sick that he barely had the energy to stand up. He was nauseous, dizzy, and dehydrated. He heard ringing in his ears, saw lights in the corners of his eyes, and suffered from hallucinations. Swallowing was excruciatingly painful for him, but he forced himself to eat in order to keep up his strength. By the end of his treatments he had lost 50 pounds, his hair had turned gray, his memory was fuzzy, and he needed a cane in order to keep his balance. Over time, though, he slowly began to regain his strength and his health.

> " The researchers concluded that participants who had more than five oral-sex partners in their lifetimes were 250 percent more likely to have throat cancer than those who did not have oral sex. "

In August 2007 Reynolds' s doctor declared him to be clean, and he and his family returned to the cottage on Cape Cod for a short vacation. Although he has no way of knowing what his long-term chances are, he is glad to have come this far and remains optimistic about the future: "I had been dreaming of this for so long," he writes. "It is what kept me moving . . . to be here, in this very moment. And when these grand two weeks are up, I find I can live with whatever happens next."[38]

Viruses That Kill

HPVs can be dangerous as well as deadly. In the past, these viruses were thought to be connected only with cervical cancer, but now researchers are finding that the risk goes far beyond that. In addition to cancer of the cervix, high-risk HPVs may lead to oral and anal cancer in both men and women, and penile cancer in men. Often, people who are diagnosed with these cancers are in a state of shock because they knew little or nothing about HPVs, and they certainly did not know about HPVs' connection with cancer. The good news is that the rising rate of HPV-connected cancer diagnoses is causing the public to be more aware of the risks associated with HPV infection. The bad news is that HPV-related cancers continue to claim thousands of lives every year.

What Are the Health Risks of Genital HPV Infection?

"High-Risk HPV Types are directly related to cervical cancer, yet many women are unaware of what HPV is or the relationship it has to cervical cancer."

—National Cervical Cancer Coalition (NCCC), "What Is the National Cervical Cancer Coalition?" 2008.

The NCCC is a grassroots organization that is dedicated to serving women with, or at risk for, cervical cancer and HPV disease.

....

"The most dangerous HPVs, 16 and 18, which are transmitted through sexual contact, are known to cause up to 95% of cervical cancers. Now these two HPVs are also being linked to oral cancer."

—Mouth Cancer Foundation (MCF), "Patient's Guide: Human Papilloma Virus," February 25, 2008. www.rdoc.org.uk

The MCF is a professional support organization in the United Kingdom that is dedicated to supporting people with mouth, throat, and other types of cancer of the head and neck.

....

* Editor's Note: While the definition of a primary source can be narrowly or broadly defined, for the purposes of Compact Research, a primary source consists of: 1) results of original research presented by an organization or researcher; 2) eyewitness accounts of events, personal experience, or work experience; 3) first-person editorials offering pundits' opinions; 4) government officials presenting political plans and/or policies; 5) representatives of organizations presenting testimony or policy.

❝The example of the relationship between HPV and cervical cancer indicates that high-risk sexual behavior and exposure to and infection with HPV will increase the risk of other cancers caused by HPV.❞

—Gypsyamber D'Souza et al., "Case Control Study of Human Papillomavirus and Oropharyngeal Cancer," *New England Journal of Medicine,* May 10, 2007. http://content.nejm.org.

D'Souza is assistant professor in the Department of Epidemiology at the Bloomberg School of Public Health.

❝Two weeks after my hysterectomy, I was watching television and saw a commercial for the HPV test and how it can help prevent cervical cancer ... I was angry that as a cervical cancer patient I didn't know about this test, or much about HPV for that matter.❞

—Kelly Cain, "Survivor Stories," Tamika & Friends, July 2005. www.tamikaandfriends.org.

Cain is a young woman who was diagnosed with cervical cancer in February 2005.

❝More severe forms of HPV can cause genital warts and penile and anal cancers. Non-genital strains can cause head and neck cancers.❞

—Tom Paulson, "New Risks Discovered for HPV," *Seattle Post-Intelligencer,* July 31, 2007. http://seattlepi.nwsource.com.

Paulson is a reporter with the *Seattle Post-Intelligencer* newspaper.

---

66 Most fortunately, and very importantly, the very great majority of HPV infections are overcome by our immune systems and resolve without further complications. 99

—Jeff Benson, "Dr. Jeff on HPV," *Bowdoin Orient,* September 30, 2005. http://orient.bowdoin.edu.

Benson is the former college physician and director of the health center at Bowdoin College in Brunswick, Maine.

66 Anal cancer is a rare occurrence that has been strongly linked to high-risk types of HPV. 99

—University Health Center, "Human Papillovirus," September 17, 2008. www.uhs.uga.edu.

The University Health Center is part of the University of Georgia, and its goal is to advance the health of students and other members of the campus community.

66 Human papillomavirus or HPV has been associated with up to 50% of the oral and throat cancers. 99

—Deborah A. Bartholomew, "HPV-Oral Cancer Risk," NetWellness, May 8, 2008, www.netwellness.org.

Bartholomew is an associate professor of obstetrics and gynecology at the Ohio State University College of Medicine.

66 Currently, there is no treatment to cure HPV. If you have it, it may live in your body forever. **99**

—Jeffrey D. Klausner, "HPV," *Ask Dr. K.*, San Francisco City Clinic, August 26, 2004. www.dph.sf.ca.us.

Klausner, an infectious disease specialist, is a deputy health officer and director of the STD Prevention and Control Services section at the San Francisco Department of Public Health.

66 The majority of cervical cancer cases, by far, are thought to result from chronic infection with certain strains of human papilloma virus (HPV) that are known to induce cancer. These high-risk strains of HPV are commonly spread through sexual contact. **99**

—Robert A. Wascher, "Human Papilloma Virus (HPV) Infection, Pap Smear Results & Cervical Cancer," *Health Report,* April 6, 2008. http://doctorwascher.com.

Wascher is an oncologic surgeon, professor of surgery, and the director of the division of surgical oncology at Newark Beth Israel Medical Center.

66 Although most Americans are aware of the part tobacco plays as a risk factor for oral cancer, few realize how serious a threat a virus such as the human papilloma virus (HPV) really is. **99**

—Manny Alvarez, "Risky Teen Behaviors Encourage Oral Cancer," FOX News, April 20, 2007. www.foxnews.com.

Alvarez is the managing editor of health news at FOXNews.com and is a regular medical contributor on the FOX News Channel.

66A patient who has had an organ transplant is at higher risk of [HPV] infections as well as cancers because of the lifelong immune suppressive medications.99

—National Institutes of Health (NIH), "Safety and Immunogenicity of Human Papillomavirus (HPV) Vaccine in Solid Organ Transplant Recipients," May 8, 2008. http://clinicaltrials.gov.

The NIH is the leading medical research organization in the United States.

66Other, different HPV types infect the skin and cause common warts elsewhere on the body. Some types of HPVs . . . frequently cause skin cancers in people who have a condition known as epidermodysplasia verruciformis.99

—Melissa Conrad Stöppler, "Human Papillomaviruses (HPVs) and Genital Warts," MedicineNet, August 22, 2006. www.medicinenet.com.

Stöppler is an anatomic pathologist and medical journalist from San Francisco.

Facts and Illustrations

What Are the Health Risks of Genital HPV Infection?

- The CDC states that in **90 percent** of the cases, the body's immune system clears HPV infection naturally within two years.

- According to the FDA, an estimated **470,000 cervical cancer** cases are diagnosed worldwide each year, and the cancer causes more than 230,000 deaths per year.

- A study announced in 2006 by researchers in Sweden found that smokers who tested positive for HPV 16 were **14.4 times** more likely to get cervical cancer than those who did not have the infection.

- A 2005 study of HIV-positive gay men in San Francisco found that **95 percent** of the men had anal HPV infection, and more than half had signs of precancerous lesions.

- The CDC reports that gay and bisexual men are **17 times more likely** to develop anal cancer than heterosexual men.

- According to the June 2005 issue of *AIDS Treatment Update*, infection with one strain of HPV **doubles a person's risk** of becoming infected with HIV, and infection with several strains more than triples the risk.

- A November 2005 case report published in *Oral Oncology Extra* states that HPV types 16 and 18 have been detected in as many as **30 percent** of oral squamous cell carcinoma (oral cancer) cases.

- The American Cancer Society predicts that more than **11,000 women** in America will be diagnosed with cervical cancer in 2008.

- The CDC states that **cervical cancer** does not have any symptoms until it is quite advanced.

- Although Pap tests have markedly reduced the number of cervical cancer deaths, studies have shown that the tests fail to identify pre-cancerous cells in about **40 percent** of cases.

A Global Epidemic

According to the American Cancer Society, cervical cancer is the second most commonly diagnosed cancer in women worldwide, with an estimated 555,100 new cases diagnosed per year and 80 percent of those cases occurring in developing countries. This map shows the international variation in cervical cancer incidence rates.

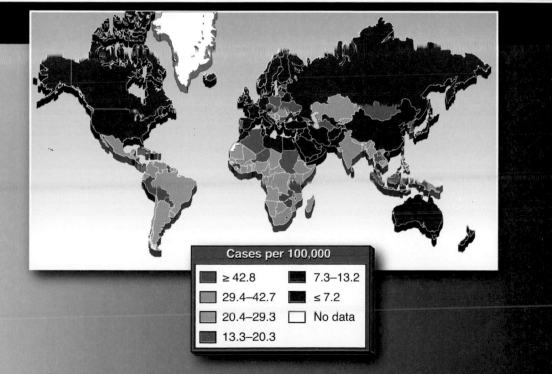

Cases per 100,000

- ≥ 42.8
- 29.4–42.7
- 20.4–29.3
- 13.3–20.3
- 7.3–13.2
- ≤ 7.2
- No data

Source: M. Garcia et al., "Global Cancer Facts & Figures 2007," American Cancer Society, 2007. www.cancer.org

Cervical Cancer in the United States

Unlike nearly all other forms of cancer, cervical cancer is caused by viruses; specifically, high-risk HPVs, most commonly types 16 and 18. In fact, high-risk HPVs are responsible for nearly 100 percent of all cervical cancer cases. This graph illustrates the prevalence of cervical cancer in the United States broken down by age.

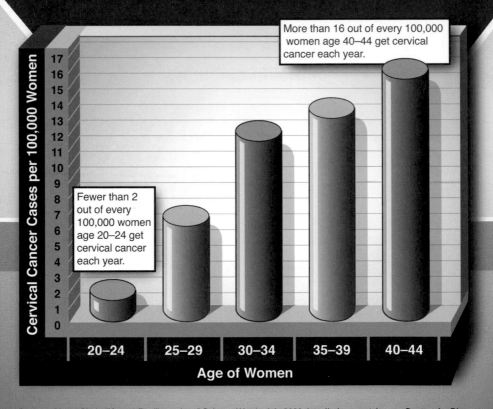

More than 16 out of every 100,000 women age 40–44 get cervical cancer each year.

Fewer than 2 out of every 100,000 women age 20–24 get cervical cancer each year.

Cervical Cancer Cases per 100,000 Women

Age of Women

Sources: Keerti Shah, "Human Papillomavirus," Science Watch, July 2008. http://sciencewatch.com; Centers for Disease Control and Prevention (CDC), "Making Sense of Your Pap and HPV Test Results," July 9, 2008. www.cdc.gov.

- The highest rate of HPV infection is among those who are between the ages of **20 and 24**.

- Health experts say that nearly **100 percent** of cervical cancer cases are caused by high-risk HPV strains, most commonly types 16 and 18.

- The CDC says that certain populations may be at higher risk of developing HPV-related cancers, including **gay and bisexual men** and those who have **weak immune systems**.

- Studies have shown that people who have had more than five oral sex partners in their lifetime are **250 percent** more likely to develop oral cancer than those who refrained from having oral sex.

HPV Vaccine's Potential to Prevent Cervical Cancer

In 2008, it is estimated that 11,070 women in the United States will get cervical cancer. In June 2008, the FDA approved Gardasil, a vaccine to prevent people from getting infection from human papillomavirus (HPV) types 6, 11, 16, and 18. HPV types 16 (HPV-16) and 18 (HPV-18) cause approximately 70 percent of cervical cancers, while HPV types 6 and 11 cause 90 percent of genital warts worldwide. Clinical trials found Gardasil to be between 95 and 100 percent effective at preventing these 4 types of HPV.

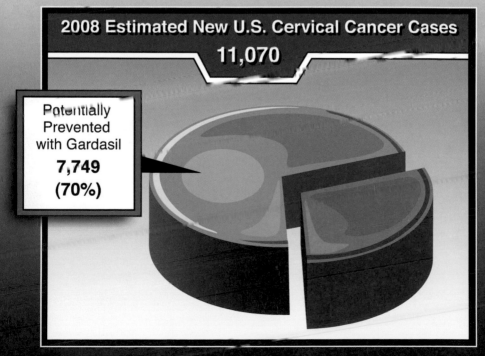

2008 Estimated New U.S. Cervical Cancer Cases
11,070

Potentially
Prevented
with Gardasil
7,749
(70%)

Disproportionate Funding

Even though the health risks of HPV are well documented, and HPV infection is, by far, the most common sexually transmitted disease, federal funding for HPV research lags far behind funding for other diseases and disorders, as this graph shows.

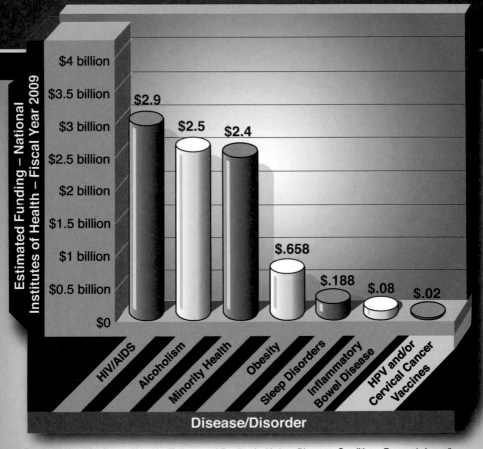

Estimated Funding – National Institutes of Health – Fiscal Year 2009

- $4 billion
- $3.5 billion
- $3 billion
- $2.5 billion
- $2 billion
- $1.5 billion
- $1 billion
- $0.5 billion
- $0

$2.9 — HIV/AIDS
$2.5 — Alcoholism
$2.4 — Minority Health
$.658 — Obesity
$.188 — Sleep Disorders
$.08 — Inflammatory Bowel Disease
$.02 — HPV and/or Cervical Cancer Vaccines

Disease/Disorder

Source: National Institutes of Health, "Estimates of Funding for Various Diseases, Conditions, Research Areas," February 5, 2008. www.nih.gov.

Should the HPV Vaccine Be Mandatory?

> **"It's really important for vaccines to be mandatory if we really want to prevent, in this case cervical cancer. . . . If you don't make a vaccine mandatory, many children will not get it. If the children don't get it, they're not protected as adults."**
>
> —Diana Zuckerman, "CNBC Interview on HPV Vaccine."

> **"Legislation to make HPV vaccine mandatory has undermined public confidence and created a backlash among parents. . . . In the absence of an immediate risk of serious harm, it is preferable to adopt voluntary measures, making state compulsion a last resort."**
>
> —Lawrence O. Gastin and Catherine D. DeAngelis, *Journal of the American Medical Association.*

Of all the people who support a mandatory requirement for the HPV vaccine, no one is more passionate about the issue than Amanda Vail. A 30-year-old graduate student from Houston, Texas, Vail was attacked and raped in December 2006 by a man who later proved to be HPV-positive. After the rape, tests showed that Vail had contracted a high-risk strain of HPV, and she was told by her doctor that she had a 70 percent chance of developing cervical cancer. Now she must have Pap tests every 3 months to check for abnormal cells—and each time, she relives the horror of the rape all over again. "I would not have to be repeatedly violated had I been vaccinated," she says. "That option wasn't available to me, and it is now available to these young women."[39]

About the Vaccine Gardasil

Although Gardasil is often referred to as a "cancer vaccine," that description is not quite accurate. What the vaccine does is guard against infection by certain HPV types. In widespread tests, Gardasil has been shown to provide nearly 100 percent protection for adolescent girls and young women against four different HPV strains: types 16 and 18, which cause 70 percent of cervical cancer cases; and types 6 and 11, which cause an estimated 90 percent of genital warts. Some studies have shown that the vaccine can protect against other HPV strains as well.

> After the rape, tests showed that Vail had contracted a high-risk strain of HPV, and she was told by her doctor that she had a 70 percent chance of developing cervical cancer.

Gardasil is a recombinant vaccine, meaning that it is produced by genetic engineering rather than made with actual viruses. According to the FDA, specific proteins that are responsible for each of the four virus types are reproduced in mass quantities, and DNA is inserted into yeast cells to make genetically engineered stock. The yeast mixture is fermented in massive vats under carefully controlled conditions, which increases cell mass and creates clones of the viruses known as VLPs (viruslike particles). These VLPs serve as the active ingredient in Gardasil. Because the vaccine contains only proteins and not live viruses, it cannot cause HPV infection once someone has been inoculated with it. The FDA explains: "It is the body's immune response to the recombinant protein(s) that then protects against infection by the naturally occurring virus."[40]

To date, Gardasil has been approved only for females aged 9 to 26. But because males and older women are also at risk for HPV infection and certain types of HPV-related cancers, studies are underway to determine the vaccine's safety and effectiveness for these groups.

State-by-State Initiatives

To cut down on the rate of HPV infection and decrease the incidents of cervical cancer, a number of states have been considering legislation that would require girls to be given the HPV vaccination. According to the National Conference of State Legislatures, as of September 2008 at least 41 states and the District of Columbia had introduced laws to require, fund, or educate the public about the HPV vaccine; and 19 of those states had enacted such legislation. In New Hampshire, for instance, the state health department announced in 2006 that it would provide the vaccine at no cost for girls under the age of 18, and as of May 2007 more than 14,000 doses were administered. In the state of Washington the legislature earmarked $10 million to voluntarily vaccinate 94,000 girls through 2009, while in North Dakota $7.5 million in federal funds were combined with $1.7 million from the state's general fund to distribute the HPV vaccine to more than 20,000 girls.

In February 2007 Texas governor Rick Perry made a bold legislative move. Perry bypassed the state legislature and issued an executive order that mandated the HPV vaccine for all girls who were entering the sixth grade. Under Perry's order, girls would be required to be vaccinated and state health authorities were obligated to make the vaccine available to girls aged 9 to 18 who were uninsured. It would also be available to women whose insurance did not cover vaccines, as well as those who were on Medicaid. In a February 5, 2007, statement, Perry defended his decision:

> " In May 2007 the Texas legislature passed House Bill 1098, which overturned the governor's order and barred mandatory HPV vaccinations until the year 2011. "

> Never before have we had an opportunity to prevent cancer with a simple vaccine. While I understand the concerns expressed by some, I stand firmly on the side of protecting life. The HPV vaccine does not promote sex, it protects women's health. In the past, young women who have abstained from sex until marriage have contracted HPV from their husbands and faced the difficult task of defeating cervical cancer. This vaccine prevents that from happening. Providing the HPV vaccine doesn't promote

sexual promiscuity anymore than providing the Hepatitis B vaccine promotes drug use. If the medical community developed a vaccine for lung cancer, would the same critics oppose it claiming it would encourage smoking?[41]

In his statement Perry referred to Amanda Vail, as well as Heather Burcham, a 31-year-old woman who was dying of cervical cancer. Burcham, whose cancer had spread to her vital organs, was growing weaker by the day. Although she was confined to a hospice facility, she had prepared a videotaped presentation to be shown after Perry's talk. Burcham honestly stated that she realized nothing more could be done for her; the cancer had spread throughout her body, she had long been in excruciating pain, and she knew she was going to die. But she made it clear that if she could reach just one person with her story and save even one single life, her suffering would not have been in vain.

Perry lost the fight for his vaccination mandate. In May 2007 the Texas legislature passed House Bill 1098, which overturned the governor's order and barred mandatory HPV vaccinations until the year 2011. Perry could have vetoed the bill, but he opted not to. Instead, he said that the legislature had made their purpose clear, and rather than open up a heated override debate, he let the bill become law without his signature. Two months later, on July 24, 2007, Heather Burcham died, and Perry paid tribute to her by speaking at her memorial service about her brave fight with cancer.

Those Who Oppose the Mandatory Vaccine

People against mandating the HPV vaccine have numerous reasons for believing the way they do. Robert Morrow, a government activist from Austin, Texas, who opposed Perry's efforts to require the vaccine, said he was offended that taxpayer money would be spent on an effort that would interfere with the rights of parents. Morrow expressed his strong views in a blistering statement in 2007: "I do not think the state of Texas should be in the business of preventative health care for teenage sluts."[42] Although many who object to the vaccine do not share Morrow's disparaging views about the young women who contract HPV, they do believe that requiring the vaccination sends the wrong message, in effect undermining sexual abstinence as the only sure way to avoid HPV infection. Leslie Unruh, founder of the National Abstinence Clearinghouse, personally objects to the vaccine because she says that HPV is 100 percent preventable if young people do not engage in improper sexual behavior.

Although some noted conservative groups such as the Family Research Council and Concerned Women for America (CWA) also strongly advocate and promote sexual abstinence, they are not against the HPV vaccine and, in fact, have spoken favorably about its potential to help prevent cervical cancer. Their concern is that once girls have been vaccinated, they may develop a false sense of security and believe that they are protected from all strains of HPV infection, which is not the case. Another concern expressed by these groups is that it is the parents' job to determine whether their child has the vaccine, rather than the government's. CWA says that making the HPV vaccine mandatory is an example of "government overreach" and that it should be a "family decision, not a state decision"[43]

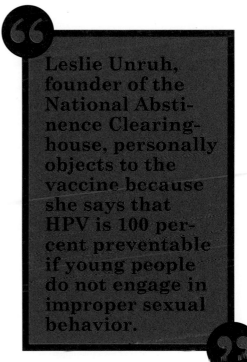

Leslie Unruh, founder of the National Abstinence Clearinghouse, personally objects to the vaccine because she says that HPV is 100 percent preventable if young people do not engage in improper sexual behavior.

Is the HPV Vaccine Safe?

One of the major arguments against making the HPV vaccine mandatory is that it has not been on the market long enough to be fully tested, and because of that, its safety is questionable. Diane M. Harper, a researcher from Dartmouth Medical School who led the development of the vaccine, says that giving it to girls as young as 11 years old "is a great big public health experiment."[44] She adds that ample evidence has not been gathered to definitively determine that the vaccine is totally safe for young girls. She says that Merck, the pharmaceutical company that sells Gardasil, has merely assumed that the vaccine would be effective in girls as young as age 9, but they do not know that for a fact. "This vaccine should not be mandated for 11-year-old girls," she says. "It's not been tested in little girls for efficacy [effectiveness]. At 11, these girls don't get cervical cancer—they won't know for 25 years if they will get cervical cancer."[45] Because of what many people believe has been insufficient testing, they are concerned that Gardasil is not safe and injections can result in serious, often permanent, side effects. Yet the FDA and CDC dispute that viewpoint. In July 2008 the agencies issued a joint statement saying that Gardasil is both safe and effective, that nearly 95 percent of all reported reactions were minor, and the benefits of the vaccine continue to outweigh the risks.

> " In June 2008 the watchdog group Judicial Watch acquired records from the FDA and issued a report stating that nearly 9,000 cases of adverse side effects and at least 18 deaths could be attributed to the HPV vaccine. "

Some people, however, will not back down in their insistence that the HPV vaccine may very likely not be safe. In June 2008 the watchdog group Judicial Watch acquired records from the FDA and issued a report stating that nearly 9,000 cases of adverse side effects and at least 18 deaths could be attributed to the HPV vaccine. "Given all the questions about Gardasil," the author writes, "the best public health policy would be to reevaluate its safety and to prohibit its distribution to minors. In the least, governments should rethink any efforts to mandate or promote this vaccine for children."[46] One young woman who suffered debilitating physical effects after being vaccinated is Jenny Tetlock. About a month after having her third Gardasil vaccination, Jenny began to experience unusual weakness in her muscles. Her condition continued to deteriorate, and over the following year paralysis gradually took its toll on her body. Today, at age 14, Jenny is a paraplegic who is confined to a wheelchair. Almost completely paralyzed, she has movement only in her neck and mouth along with a slight ability to move her left hand, and even breathing is an ongoing struggle for her. Jenny's family believes the HPV vaccination is linked to her mysterious illness, but they have not been able to prove it.

A similar tragedy struck a teenage girl named Amanda. In July 2008 journalist Sharyl Attkisson interviewed Amanda's parents, both of whom are physicians, and she learned that they also suspect that Gardasil was responsible for their daughter's debilitating illness. After Amanda received her first vaccination about a year ago, her arm was initially sore at the site of the injection, which is common. But then the soreness began to creep down her arm, and then down her legs, and over time Amanda was stricken with an autoimmune disease that caused her so much pain she had to regularly take morphine. Attkisson explains the end result: "She was transformed, through the illness, from a high school varsity sport athlete to a chronically ill person who takes a handful of pills a day just to keep her illness tolerable. When she goes off the medicine, the excruciating pain and other debilitating symptoms return."[47] As with the Tetlocks, Amanda's parents can only speculate about whether their daughter's condition is a direct result of her Gardasil injection. But because she was so healthy before the vaccine, they cannot help but be suspicious.

The HPV Vaccine Mired in Controversy

The debate over the HPV vaccine continues to rage on with no end in sight. One side argues that the vaccine should be required because it has the potential to save thousands of lives that are now needlessly lost to cervical cancer. The other side argues that the vaccine needs further testing before it can be ruled 100 percent safe, and they punctuate their arguments with statistics of young women who have developed mysterious, life-threatening ailments soon after being vaccinated. Still others insist that the vaccine itself sends the wrong message because it flies in the face of the sexual abstinence message and could encourage promiscuity. So where will it all end? Will there eventually be a common ground? No one can answer those questions for sure. But because HPV has clearly been shown to be the most prevalent sexually transmitted infection in the world—and every day of the year it continues to infect thousands of women and men, many of whom die from cancers related to the viruses—one can only hope that this debate will be resolved sometime in the very near future.

Should the HPV Vaccine Be Mandatory?

66 And what if your daughter is as pure as the driven snow, waits to have sex until she's married, and gets infected on her wedding night by a man who has HPV? What if it isn't caught in time, because she's certain that she's 'been a good girl' so she believes there's no chance of contracting any STDs? . . . The vaccine should be mandatory, and no parent should be allowed to keep their daughter from obtaining it.**99**

—Audree Tucker, "Why the HPV Vaccine Should Be Mandatory," *Helium,* 2007. www.helium.com.

Tucker is a writer and former political consultant from the Tampa Bay area in Florida.

66 No list of talking points can justify forcing this vaccine on schoolchildren for a disease that is not contagious in the classroom environment.**99**

—Phyllis Schlafly, "Experimenting on Teen Girls," Eagle Forum, March 7, 2007. www.eagleforum.org.

Schlafly is a conservative political activist and author who is known for her organized opposition to the Equal Rights Amendment.

Bracketed quotes indicate conflicting positions.

* Editor's Note: While the definition of a primary source can be narrowly or broadly defined, for the purposes of Compact Research, a primary source consists of: 1) results of original research presented by an organization or researcher; 2) eyewitness accounts of events, personal experience, or work experience; 3) first-person editorials offering pundits' opinions; 4) government officials presenting political plans and/or policies; 5) representatives of organizations presenting testimony or policy.

66 People don't get the vaccine for typhoid and say, 'Great, now I can drink the sewer water in Bombay.' . . . It's like being against a cure for blindness because it'll encourage masturbation. 99

—Bill Maher, "Bill Maher on the HPV Vaccine," Shapes and Shores blog, March 10, 2007. http://pier900.blogspot.com.

Maher is an Emmy-winning actor, comedian, and political commentator.

66 If conservatives are right that the [HPV] vaccine sends a mixed message, then all the more reason to make it mandatory. That would allow concerned parents who favor abstinence to trust . . . but verify. And to explain that they're doing this for the larger good of the whole herd. 99

—Nancy Gibbs, "Diffusing the War over the 'Promiscuity' Vaccine," *Time,* June 21, 2006. www.time.com.

Gibbs is an editor-at-large for *Time* magazine.

66 Assuming the [HPV vaccine] is safe, vaccination should be the parents' option to choose for their daughters or for women to choose for themselves. . . . Medical decisions should be between patient and provider and any intrusion without a significant government interest is unconstitutional. 99

—John Bambenek, "Invasion of Privacy: State Has No Business Mandating HPV Vaccine," *Blog Critics Magazine,* January 25, 2007. http://blogcritics.org.

Bambenek is an information security practitioner and opinions columnist from Champaign, Illinois.

66 Some overprotective parents contend that girls will have more sex because this vaccination protects them from cervical cancer; this is completely untrue. . . . The idea that teens would become more sexually active just because they got a shot is ridiculous! 99

—Samantha Richards, "HPV Vaccine: A Shot of Prevention," *LA Youth,* May/June 2007. www.layouth.com.

Richards is a teenage girl from Los Angeles.

66 We're going to be sending a message to a lot of kids, I think, that you just take this shot and you can be as sexually promiscuous as you want and it's not going to be a problem, and that's just not true. 99

—Hal Wallis, quoted in Ronald Bailey, "Safety, Efficacy, Morality," *Reason,* November 4, 2005. www.reason.com.

Wallis is chairman of the Physicians Consortium and a medical adviser for several abstinence education programs.

66 Would giving the vaccine encourage promiscuity? Unlikely, based on prior studies about the availability of free condoms. Would withholding the vaccine prevent promiscuity? Unlikely, based on the fact that the threat of HIV has not stopped it. 99

—Rima Bishara, "The HPV Vaccine and Its Implications," Doctor Blogger, May 23, 2007. http://thedoctorblogger.com.

Bishara is a physician from Waco, Texas, who specializes in internal medicine.

> 66 Regarding side effects, there haven't been any serious side effects observed to date with the [HPV] vaccine. Of those observed, pain and swelling at the site of the injection are the most common. 99

—Richard Schlegel, "HPV Vaccine," *Washington Post,* January 17, 2007. www.washingtonpost.com.

Schlegel, who has studied HPV for 25 years, is chair of the Georgetown University Medical Center's Department of Pathology.

> 66 So far, more than four million [HPV] vaccinations have been done and nearly 4,000 adverse reactions have been reported. . . . The list of complaints range from temporary blindness, blurry vision, convulsions, seizures and numbness in arms and legs that won't go away. 99

—Jakelyn Barnard, "Mom Says HPV Vaccine Caused Paralysis in 12-Year-Old," *First Coast News*, November 13, 2007. www.firstcoastnews.com.

Barnard is chief investigative reporter for the Jacksonville, Florida, *First Coast News.*

> 66 It is exciting to think that a simple vaccination could bring cervical cancer rates around the world down to the levels seen in developed countries today, or even lower. Now that the role of HPV in cervical cancer is known, prevention is a real possibility. 99

—Susan C. Stewart, "Human Papilloma Virus and Cervical Cancer," The Doctor Will See You Now, May 2006. www.thedoctorwillseeyounow.com.

Stewart is the chair of the American Medical Women's Association health committee and a clinical assistant professor of medicine at New York Medical College.

66There is no doubt that many well-intentioned parents out there are being deceived, or at the least seriously misled . . . into believing that Gardasil is beneficial for their daughters. . . . This vaccine campaign is so high on hyped-up fear and so deficient in logic, it boggles the mind.99

—Joseph Mercola, "HPV Vaccine: The Truth Is, Your Daughters DO NOT NEED This Vaccine!" libNOT, September 9, 2008. www.libnot.com.

Mercola is a physician and author who specializes in natural medicine education.

....

66Taking steps to encourage abstinence should definitely be encouraged, but there is no research that a vaccine will encourage more teens to have sex or have more partners.99

—Vincent Iannelli, "HPV Controversy," About.com Pediatrics, May 10, 2007. http://pediatrics.about.com.

Iannelli is a pediatrician and fellow of the American Academy of Pediatrics. He lives in Dallas, Texas.

....

Facts and Illustrations

Should the HPV Vaccine Be Mandatory?

- In 1984, 20 years after German virologist **Harald zur Hausen** discovered the link between HPV and cervical cancer, he tried to convince pharmaceutical companies to develop an HPV vaccine, but they refused, saying that the problem was not urgent enough.

- **Gardasil**, manufactured by the pharmaceutical company Merck, is currently the only approved vaccine in the United States to protect against HPV.

- Gardasil protects against HPV types 16 and 18, which cause more than **70 percent** of cervical cancers, as well as types 6 and 11, which are responsible for an estimated **90 percent** of genital warts.

- Medical audits that were conducted 24 months after the FDA approved Gardasil found that only **17 percent** of the surveyed physicians had administered the vaccine; the same audits found that as of the first quarter of 2008, only **10 percent** of girls and young women aged 9 to 26 had been vaccinated, and only **2 percent** had completed the recommended 3-dose regimen.

- According to the FDA, more than **10,500** females who received Gardasil were evaluated for adverse reactions, and the majority of them were limited to mild or moderate pain or tenderness at the site of the injection.

Parental Opinions on Mandating the HPV Vaccine

In June 2006 a vaccine called Gardasil was approved by the U.S. Food and Drug Administration (FDA) for adolescent girls and women ages 9 to 26. The vaccine protects against 4 strains of HPV that are responsible for 70 percent of cervical cancers and at least 90 percent of genital warts. In a survey published in May 2007 by the University of Michigan's C.S. Mott Children's Hospital, parents from 48 states and the District of Columbia were asked:

Would you support a state law that requires girls to receive the HPV vaccine before entering the ninth grade?

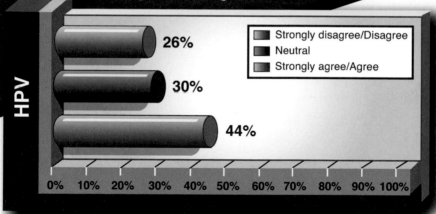

Would you support a state law requiring boys and girls to get a new booster vaccine that protects against tetanus, diphtheria, and whooping cough (Tdap) before entering ninth grade?

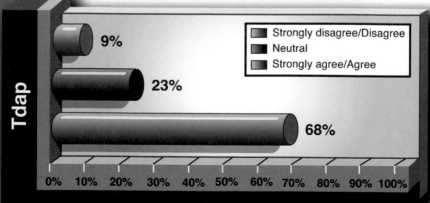

Source: C.S. Mott Children's Hospital, "National Poll on Children's Health," May 22, 2007. www.med.umich.edu.

Physicians' Recommendations on HPV Vaccine

A survey that was published in the December 2006 issue of *Pediatrics* examined the attitudes of pediatricians about the HPV vaccination. This graph illustrates what the physicians said when asked how likely they would be to recommend the vaccine for females in various age groups.

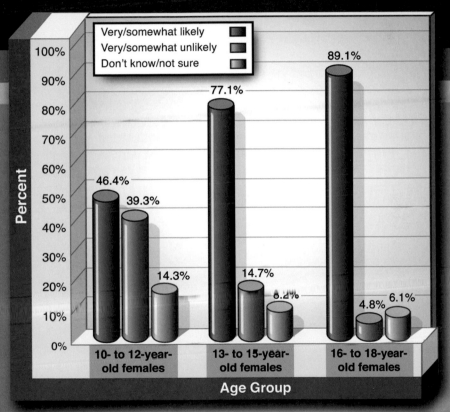

Source: Matthew M. Daley et al., "A National Survey of Pediatrician Knowledge and Attitudes Regarding Human Papillomavirus Vaccination," *Pediatrics*, December 2006. http://pediatrics.aappublications.org.

- A study published in November 2008 showed that Gardasil was **safe for males**, and was effective at cutting infections by the four most dangerous HPV strains by **45 percent**, as well as reducing the occurrence of genital warts by **90 percent**. FDA approval is pending.

- **Texas** was the first state with an **executive order** mandating that the HPV vaccine be given to girls entering the sixth grade, but the state legislature overturned the order in May 2007.

- The HPV vaccine is not effective in someone who is **already infected** with types 6, 11, 16, and/or 18.

State-by-State Legislation

In an effort to decrease the spread of HPV infection and reduce the incidence of cervical cancer, a number of states have been considering legislation that would either require girls to be vaccinated against HPV, enact measures that would finance vaccinations, and/or pay for educational material about vaccinations. This map shows the states where various legislative moves have been enacted or proposed as of September 2008.

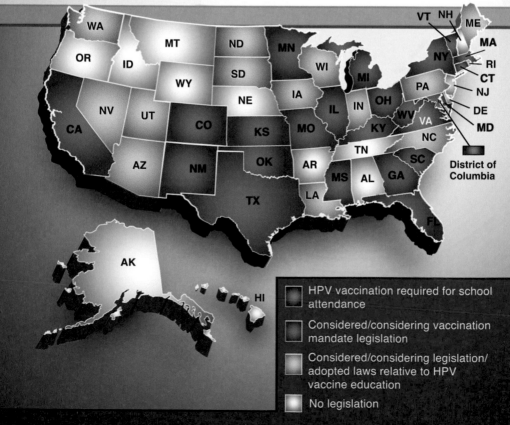

- HPV vaccination required for school attendance
- Considered/considering vaccination mandate legislation
- Considered/considering legislation/adopted laws relative to HPV vaccine education
- No legislation

Source: Victoria Stagg Elliott, "HPV Vaccine Talk Shifts from Fanfare to Fear," American Medical News, September 15, 2008. www.ama-assn.org.

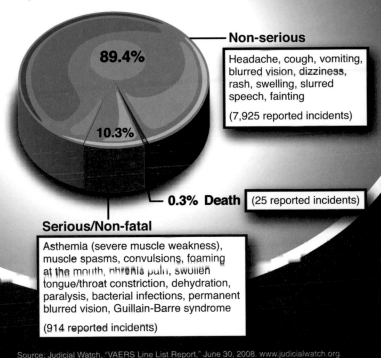

HPV Vaccine Safety

Although tests have shown that Gardasil is safe and effective as protection against at least four strains of HPV, there have been numerous reports of serious physical ailments that struck young women after the vaccine was administered. Using information provided through the Freedom of Information Act, Judicial Watch examined a total of 8,864 Vaccine Adverse Event Reporting System (VAERS) reports submitted by medical providers and the group compiled statistics about adverse reactions.

89.4%

Non-serious

Headache, cough, vomiting, blurred vision, dizziness, rash, swelling, slurred speech, fainting

(7,925 reported incidents)

10.3%

0.3% Death (25 reported incidents)

Serious/Non-fatal

Asthemia (severe muscle weakness), muscle spasms, convulsions, foaming at the mouth, chronic pain, swollen tongue/throat constriction, dehydration, paralysis, bacterial infections, permanent blurred vision, Guillain-Barre syndrome

(914 reported incidents)

Source: Judicial Watch, "VAERS Line List Report," June 30, 2008. www.judicialwatch.org.

- Many experts on vaccinations have recommended that **all girls** should get the HPV vaccine when they are 11 or 12 years old; girls and women between 13 and 26 can also benefit from the vaccine if they are not HPV-positive.

- The American Medical Association (AMA) supports the **HPV vaccine** but is against making it mandatory.

Key People and Advocacy Groups

Centers for Disease Control and Prevention (CDC): The CDC is a federal government agency that seeks to promote health and quality of life by controlling disease, injury, and disability, and which recommends the HPV vaccine for females aged 11 through 26.

Concerned Women for America (CWA): The CWA is a women's organization that seeks to bring biblical principles into all levels of public policy and has spoken out publicly against mandating the HPV vaccine for girls.

Food and Drug Administration (FDA): The FDA is an organization charged with keeping products safe and effective, monitoring products for continued safety once they are in use, and providing the public with accurate, science-based information. In 2006 an FDA advisory committee ruled 13 to 0 that the HPV vaccine Gardasil was safe and effective for females aged 9 to 26.

Harald zur Hausen: A German virologist, zur Hausen is known as a pioneer in the field of HPV research.

Merck & Co., Inc.: Merck is the manufacturer of the vaccine Gardasil, which protects against four types of HPVs that cause an estimated 70 percent of cervical cancer cases.

George Papanicolaou: In 1928 Papanicolaou, a scientist originally from Greece, developed the Pap test, a diagnostic test that is widely used to detect cervical cancer in women.

Rick Perry: Perry is the Texas governor who in February 2007 issued an executive order requiring that all female students be vaccinated against HPV before entering the sixth grade.

Planned Parenthood Federation of America: The federation provides health-care services, sex education, and sexual health information to women, men, and young people throughout the United States.

Ernst Ruska: A German scientist, Ruska invented the electron microscope, which made it possible to observe viruses and other objects that were too small to be viewed with ordinary microscopes.

Keerti Shah: In 1999 Shah, a virologist, announced that 99.7 percent of cervical cancer cases are caused by HPV infection.

Richard E. Shope: A scientist from Iowa, Shope was the first to isolate the papillomavirus in cottontail rabbits and observe that the virus induced warts.

Elizabeth Stern: A Canadian pathologist, Stern was the first to link a specific virus (herpes simplex) to a specific cancer (cervical cancer). Although her theory about the virus was incorrect, she has been lauded for research that led to better diagnostic tests for early detection and treatment of cervical cancer.

Chronology

1931
German scientist Ernst Ruska invents the electron microscope, which makes it possible to view objects too small to be seen with ordinary microscopes, including viruses, proteins, and atoms.

1842
Italian physician and statistician Domenico Rigoni-Stern reports that married women have a much higher rate of cervical cancer than celibate nuns, in whom the disease is virtually nonexistent; he hypothesizes that the cancer is sexually transmitted.

1935
Scientists Peyton Rous and J.W. Beard discover that when warts induced in rabbits grow unchecked, some become malignant.

1898
Dutch scientist Martinus Willem Beijerinck is the first to use the word *virus* to describe a seemingly invisible organism that infects tobacco plants.

1880   1900   1920   1940   1960

1907
The viral nature of human warts is discovered by Italian physician Ciuffo.

1963
Canadian pathologist Elizabeth Stern becomes the first to link a specific virus (herpes simplex) to a specific cancer (cervical cancer). The virus is later determined to be HPV, but Stern's research leads to better diagnostic tests for early detection and treatment of cervical cancer.

1928
After studying cancer cells on vaginal smears from female animals, American scientist George Papanicolaou uses the same technique on human females; the diagnostic method he develops, which is used to detect cervical cancer in women, is named the Pap test.

1933
American scientist Richard Shope becomes the first to isolate the papillomavirus in cottontail rabbits and observe that the virus induces warts.

1970
Using an electron microscope, scientists J.D. Oriel and June Almeida discover virus particles in human genital warts, and publish a paper about their findings in the *British Journal of Venereal Diseases.*

1991
Development of a vaccine against HPV begins; viruslike particles from the papillomavirus are isolated and injected into animals, which is shown to protect against the formation of warts.

2008
The Centers for Disease Control and Prevention (CDC) announces that one in four female adolescents in the United States has at least one sexually transmitted infection, most commonly HPV.

November: a two-year study is released, showing that Gardasil is safe for males as well as females, and is effective in cutting infections by the four most dangerous HPV strains by 45 percent, as well as reducing the occurence of genital warts by 90 percent.

1970　　　　1980　　　　1990　　　　2000　　　　2010

1983
German scientists Harald zur Hausen and Lutz Gissmann show the relationship of HPV 16 and HPV 18 to cervical cancer; many other scientists reject the theory.

1999
After investigating the prevalence of HPV in women from 22 countries, virologist Keerti Shah and his colleagues announce that HPV accounts for 99.7 percent of cervical cancer cases.

2001
After clinical trials, the HPV vaccine Gardasil is determined to be effective in protecting against HPV types 16, 18, 6, and 11.

2007
Texas governor Rick Perry issues an executive order requiring that girls entering the sixth grade be vaccinated for HPV; the Texas legislature passes a bill that overrides the governor's order.

2006
The Food and Drug Administration (FDA) approves Gardasil for use in females ages 9 to 26.

Related Organizations

American Cancer Society (ACS)
National Headquarters
250 Williams St.
Atlanta, GA 30303
phone: (800) 227-2345
Web site: www.cancer.org

ACS is a health organization that is dedicated to eliminating cancer as a major health problem through research, education, advocacy, and service. Its Web site offers frequently asked questions about HPV, a searchable glossary, numerous fact sheets, statistics, and news stories.

American College of Obstetricians and Gynecologists (ACOG)
409 12th St. SW
PO Box 96920
Washington, DC 20090-6920
phone: (202) 638-5577
Web site: www.acog.org

ACOG, which has more than 50,000 members, serves as an advocate for quality health care for women. Its Web site offers numerous publications related to HPV, such as fact sheets for teens, news releases, information about the HPV vaccine, and educational pamphlets.

American Medical Association (AMA)
515 N. State St.
Chicago, IL 60610
phone: (312) 464-5199; toll-free: (800) 621-8335
fax: (312) 464-5900
e-mail: info@ama-assn.org
Web site: www.ama-assn.org

The AMA's mission is to promote the art and science of medicine and the betterment of public health. Its Web site offers a wide variety of materials such as speech transcripts, news releases, articles, and the *American Medical News* newsletter.

American Social Health Association (ASHA)
PO Box 13827
Research Triangle Park, NC 27709
phone: (919) 361-8400
fax: (919) 361-8425
e-mail: info@ashastd.org
Web site: www.ashastd.org

ASHA is dedicated to improving the health of individuals, families, and communities, with a focus on education to help prevent and destigmatize sexually transmitted diseases. Its Web site offers news releases, fact sheets, and reports, along with a number of other HPV publications that are available for purchase.

Centers for Disease Control and Prevention (CDC)
1600 Clifton Rd.
Atlanta, GA 30333
phone: (404) 498-1515; toll-free: (800) 311-3435
fax: (800) 553-6323
e-mail: inquiry@cdc.gov
Web site: www.cdc.gov

The CDC is charged with promoting health and quality of life by controlling disease, injury, and disability. Its Web site offers HPV information sheets, facts and statistics about HPV, and downloadable brochures and posters.

Concerned Women for America (CWA)
1015 15th St, NW, Suite 1100
Washington, DC 20005
phone: (202) 488-7000
fax: (202) 488-0806
Web site: www.cwfa.org

CWA is a women's organization that seeks to bring biblical principles into all levels of public policy. Its Web site offers HPV fact sheets, papers about the HPV vaccine, and articles.

Family Research Council (FRC)
801 G St. NW
Washington, DC 20001
phone: (202) 393-2100
fax: (202) 393-2134
Web site: www.frc.org

The FRC is dedicated to the promotion of marriage and family and the sanctity of human life in national policy. Its Web site offers information about teen sexual abstinence, HPV, and the HPV vaccine, as well as news releases.

Food and Drug Administration (FDA)
5600 Fishers Ln.
Rockville, MD 20857
phone: (888) 463-6332
Web site: www.fda.gov

The FDA is charged with promoting and protecting the public health by keeping products safe and effective, monitoring products for continued safety once they are in use, and providing the public with accurate, science-based information. Materials available on the Web site include HPV fact sheets, information about cervical cancer screening and the HPV vaccine, and consumer updates.

Judicial Watch
501 School St. SW, Suite 500
Washington, DC 20024
phone: (888) 593-8442
fax: (202) 646-5199

e-mail: info@judicialwatch.org
Web site: www.judicialwatch.org

Judicial Watch is a conservative, nonpartisan educational foundation that promotes transparency, accountability, and integrity in government, politics, and the law. Its Web site features news releases, investigative reports, and a link to the *Corruption Chronicles* blog.

Mayo Clinic
200 First St. SW
Rochester, MN 55905
phone: (507) 284-2511
fax: (507) 284-0161
Web site: ww.mayoclinic.com

The Mayo Clinic is a world-renowned medical practice that is dedicated to the diagnosis and treatment of virtually every type of complex illness and disease. Available on its Web site are numerous publications related to HPV infection, common and genital warts, cervical cancer, the HPV vaccine, and HPV tests.

National Cervical Cancer Coalition (NCCC)
6520 Platt Ave. #693
West Hills, CA 91307
phone: (818) 909-3849; toll-free: (800) 685-5531
fax: (818) 780-8199
e-mail: info@nccc-online.org
Web site: www.nccc-online.org

The NCCC is a growing coalition of people who seek to battle cervical cancer and address HPV-related issues. Its Web site offers health articles available through a searchable database, cervical cancer and HPV topics, survivor stories, and a quarterly *Extraordinary Moments* newsletter.

National Institutes of Health (NIH)
9000 Rockville Pike
Bethesda, MD 20892

phone: (301) 496-4000
e-mail: NIHinfo@od.nih.gov
Web site: www.nih.gov

The NIH, the leading medical research organization in the United States, is the primary federal agency for conducting and supporting medical research. NIH scientists search for ways to improve human health as well as investigate the causes, treatments, and possible cures for diseases. Its Web site offers a wide variety of materials about HPV including fact sheets, current studies and research findings, news articles, and links to other HPV-related publications.

Planned Parenthood Federation of America (PPFA)

434 W. 33rd St.
New York, NY 10001
phone: (212) 541-7800; toll free: (800) 230-7526
fax: (212) 245-1845
Web site: www.plannedparenthood.org

Through its network of 99 affiliates that operate nearly 900 health centers, PPFA provides health-care services, sex education, and sexual health information to women, men, and young people. Its Web site offers numerous publications about what HPV is, its symptoms, its connection with cervical warts and cancer, and the HPV vaccine.

For Further Research

Books

William Bonnez, ed., *Guide to Genital HPV Infection.* London, UK: Informa Healthcare, 2008.

Larry H. Gregory, *Are You at Risk for a Cancer from HPV?* Westerville, OH: Gregory & Co., 2005.

Gregory Henderson and Batya Swift Yasgur, *Women at Risk: The HPV Epidemic and Your Cervical Health.* New York: Avery, 2002.

Shobha S. Krishnan, *The HPV Vaccine Controversy.* Westport, CT: Praeger, 2008.

Lisa Marr, *Sexually Transmitted Diseases: A Physician Tells You What You Need to Know.* Baltimore: Johns Hopkins University Press, 2007.

Joseph Monsonégo, *Emerging Issues on HPV Infections.* New York: Karger, 2006.

Adina Nack, *Damaged Goods? Women Living with Incurable Sexually Transmitted Diseases.* Philadelphia, Temple University Press, 2008.

Don Nardo, *Human Papillomavirus (HPV).* Detroit: Lucent, 2007.

Joel Palefsky and Jody Handley, *What Your Doctor May Not Tell You About HPV and Abnormal Pap Smears.* New York: Warner, 2002.

James N. Parker and Philip M. Parker, eds., *Genital HPV Infection.* San Diego, CA: Icon, 2002.

Alvin Silverstein, Virginia Silverstein, and Laura Silverstein Nunn, *The STDs Update.* Berkeley Heights, NJ: Enslow, 2006.

Periodicals

M. Natalie Achong, "What Women Need to Know About HPV and Cervical Cancer," *Ebony*, July 2007.

Alicia M. Bell, "Hold the Hype on HPV," *Women's Health Activist*, May/June 2007.

Heather Boerner, "Get the Shot: The HPV Vaccine Isn't Just for Straight Girls," *Curve*, January/February 2007.

Doug Brunk, "Expert Outlines Why Universal HPV Vaccination Is Needed," *Family Practice News*, August 15, 2008.

Margena A. Christian, "Why African-American Girls Are Infected with STDs at Higher Rates," *Jet*, April 14, 2008.

Concerned Women for America, "HPV: Highly Politicized Vaccine," *CWA Family Voice*, May/June 2007.

Victoria Stagg Elliott, "Dr. Pap's Smear: The Test and Its Times," *American Medical News*, September 3, 2007.

————, "Plans Sought to Curb Teen Girls' High STD Rate," *American Medical News*, April 14, 2008.

Alexis Jetter, "The Hot Shot," *Vogue*, May 2007.

Melissa Ewey Johnson, "Safe Sex 101: Intimate Knowledge," *Essence*, February 2008.

Anne Lang, "Should 6th Graders Get the HPV Shot—by Law?" *People Weekly*, April 2, 2007.

Elissa Mendenhall, "Guard Against Gardasil," *Mothering*, May/June 2007.

Claire Cain Miller, "The Cancer That Shouldn't Be," *Forbes*, January 28, 2008.

Kate O'Beirne, "A Mandate in Texas: The Story of a Compulsory Vaccination and What It Means," *National Review*, March 5, 2007.

Gail O'Connor, "I Have an STD. Now What?" *Cosmopolitan*, December 2007.

Lindsey O'Connor, "The HPV Vaccine: Should Your Daughter Get This Controversial New Immunization?" *Today's Christian Woman*, July/August 2007.

Kevin B. O'Reilly, "Will States Follow Texas on HPV Shot Mandate?" *American Medical News*, February 26, 2007.

Stephen Reynolds, "A Father's Brave Battle with Throat Cancer," *Reader's Digest*, August 2008.

Tara Roberts, "The Truth About STDs," *Cosmopolitan*, April 2008.

Julia Scirrotto, "Sex, Lies, and the HPV Vaccine," *Marie Claire*, February 2008.

Hallie Levine Sklar, "The Most Dangerous STD Threat to Women," *Cosmopolitan*, December 2006.

Hannah Wallace, "Infection Protection: A Strong Immune System and Lifestyle Changes Can Help Control HPV—and Keep Cervical Cancer at Bay," *Natural Health*, October 2007.

Claudia Wallis, "Saying Yes to the Shot," *Time*, March 19, 2007.

Emily Kate Warren, "What the Heck Is HPV?" *CosmoGirl*, September 2006.

Sarah Webb, "A Shot of Prevention: Vaccines That Teens Need to Stay Healthy," *Current Health 2, a Weekly Reader Publication*, September 2008.

Internet Sources

American Cancer Society, "Frequently Asked Questions About Human Papilloma Virus (HPV) Vaccines," December 4, 2007. www.cancer. org/docroot/CRI/content/CRI_2_6x_FAQ_HP V_Vaccines. asp.

Centers for Disease Control and Prevention, "Genital HPV Infection," December 2007. www.cdc.gov/std/HPV/hpv-fact-sheet.pdf.

———, "HPV and Men," December 2007. www.cdc.gov/STD/HPV/ HPV&Men-Fact-Sheet.pdf.

Food and Drug Administration (FDA) Office of Women's Health, "HPV (Human Papillomavirus)," June 2006. www.fda.gov/womens/getthe facts/pdfs/hpv.pdf.

Glenn Gandelman, "Genital Warts," review, How Stuff Works, February 8, 2007. http://healthguide.howstuffworks.com/genital-warts-diction ary.htm.

Denise Grady, "A Vital Discussion, Clouded," *New York Times*, March 6, 2007. www.nytimes.com/2007/03/06/health/06seco.html.

Mitchell Hecht, "Ask Dr. H: The Causes and the Cures for Warts," *Philadelphia Inquirer*, June 30, 2008. www.philly.com/inquirer/columnists/ mitchell_hecht/20080630_Ask_Dr_H_The_causes_and_the_cures_ for_warts.html.

Douglas Holt, "HPV Vaccine: A Little Pain Now, Cancer Protection Later," ABC News, January 7, 2008. http://hscweb3.hsc.usf.edu/health/ now/?p=322.

Deborah Kotz, "Is HPV Vaccine to Blame for a Teen's Paralysis?" *U.S. News & World Report*, July 2, 2008. www.usnews.com/blogs/on-wom en/2008/7/2/is-hpv-vaccine-to-blame-for-a-teens-paralysis.html.

Mayo Clinic, "HPV Infection," July 1, 2008. www.mayoclinic.com/health/ hpv-infection/DS00906.

National Institutes of Health (NIH), "Safety and Immunogenicity of Human Papillomavirus (HPV) Vaccine in Solid Organ Transplant

Recipients," May 8, 2008. http://clinicaltrials.gov/ct2/show/NCT00 677677?term=vaccine+adverse+reactions&recr=open&rank=12.

Planned Parenthood, "HPV," February 21, 2008. www.plannedparent hood.org/health-topics/stds-hiv-safer-sex/hpv-4272.htm.

Mike Stobbe, "HPV Causing More Oral Cancer in Men," *USA Today*, February 2, 2008. www.usatoday.com/news/health/2008-02-01-hpv-cancer_N.htm

Janet M. Torpy, "Human Papillomavirus Infection," *Journal of the American Medical Association*, February 28, 2007. http://jama.ama-assn.org/cgi/reprint/297/8/912.

Source Notes

Overview

1. Arianna Daut, "I Have an STD. Now What?" *Cosmopolitan*, December 2007, p. 209.
2. Daut, "I Have an STD. Now What?"
3. Daut, "I Have an STD. Now What?"
4. Quoted in Cindy Bevington, "Researcher Blasts HPV Marketing," *Fort Wayne Daily News*, March 14, 2007. www.kpcnews.com.
5. American Cancer Society, "Frequently Asked Questions About Human Papilloma Virus (HPV) Vaccines," December 4, 2007. www.cancer.org.
6. American Social Health Association, "Emotional Solitaire," 2007. www.ashastd.org.
7. Mayo Clinic, "HPV Infection," March 13, 2007. www.mayoclinic.com.
8. Quoted in Denise Grady, "A Vital Discussion, Clouded," *New York Times*, March 6, 2007. www.nytimes.com.
9. Margaret J. Meeker, "Risky Business: An Interview with Dr. Meg Meeker," *That's Where I Live*, January 2006. www.lifeathletes.org.
10. Anonymous, "Living with HPV," *AIDS Treatment Update*, November 2005. www.aidsmap.com.
11. Anonymous, "Living with HPV."
12. Quoted in Grady, "A Vital Discussion, Clouded."
13. Meeker, "Risky Business: An Interview with Dr. Meg Meeker."
14. Quoted in Janet Guyon, "The Coming Storm over a Cancer Vaccine," *Fortune*, October 31, 2005. http://money.cnn.com.
15. Nancy Gibbs, "Diffusing the War over the 'Promiscuity' Vaccine," *Time*, June 21, 2006. www.time.com.

What Is HPV?

16. Richard E. Shope, "Infectious Papillomatosis of Rabbits," *Journal of Experimental Medicine*, July 19, 1933. www.jem.org.
17. Shope, "Infectious Papillomatosis of Rabbits."
18. Corey Binns, "Inside Look: How Viruses Invade Us," Live Science, June 5, 2006. www.livescience.com.
19. Joel Palefsky, "HPV: Bare-Bones Basics," NotAlone, 2002. www.enotalone.com.
20. Kath Mazzella, "Kath's Story—a Personal Experience with HPV," *Australian Health Consumer*, 2003–2004. www.chf.org.au.
21. Quoted in Matthew Moore, "Tree Man 'Who Grew Roots' May Be Cured," *Telegraph*, August 27, 2008. www.telegraph.co.uk.

What Causes HPV Infection?

22. Ed Rybicki, "Where Do Viruses Come From?" *Scientific American*, March 27, 2008. www.sciam.com.
23. Palefsky, "HPV: Bare-Bones Basics."
24. Palefsky, "HPV: Bare-Bones Basics."
25. Kathy Greaves, "Virgins Beware: STIs Can Still Be There," *Daily Barometer*, April 9, 2003. http://media.barometer.orst.edu.
26. Quoted in Jenny Shearer, "STDs Raise Risks Beyond Intercourse," *Spartan Daily*, November 14, 2003. www.thespartandaily.com.
27. Julie Gerberding, "Report to Congress: Prevention of Genital Human Papillomavirus," January 2004. www.cdc.gov.
28. Anonymous, "A Moment of Unprotected Sex Leads to HPV," Sex, etc.,

posted March 18, 2004; revised October 25, 2006. www.sexetc.org.

29. Anonymous, "A Moment of Unprotected Sex Leads to HPV."

30. Richard Schlegel, "HPV Vaccine," *Washington Post*, January 17, 2007. www.washingtonpost.com.

What Are the Health Risks of Genital HPV Infection?

31. Peter McIntyre, "Finding the Viral Link: The Story of Harald zur Hausen," *Cancer World*, July/August 2005, p. 35.

32. Frances Masterman, "I Stood Up to My Doctor," in Kristyn Kusek, "My Tipping Point," *More*, April 2006. www.thehpvtest.com.

33. Quoted in Claire Amber Young, "Cancer Mum: Baby Saved My Live," *Greenock Telegraph*, August 30, 2008. www.greenocktelegraph.co.uk.

34. Liz Ellwood, "HPV and Cervical Cancer: One Woman's Story," Med Broadcast, 2007. www.medbroadcast.com.

35. Quoted in Coco Masters, "Oral Sex Can Add to HPV Cancer Risk," *Time*, May 11, 2007. www.time.com.

36. Stephen Reynolds, "A Father's Brave Battle with Throat Cancer," *Reader's Digest*, August 2008, p. 175.

37. Reynolds, "A Father's Brave Battle with Throat Cancer," p. 178.

38. Reynolds, "A Father's Brave Battle with Throat Cancer," p. 188.

Should the HPV Vaccine Be Mandatory?

39. Quoted in *Fort Bend Herald* (Fort Bend, TX), "Lawmakers Discuss Requiring Cervical Cancer Vaccine," February 20, 2007. www.herald-coaster.com.

40. U.S. Food and Drug Administration, "GARDASIL® Questions and Answers," June 8, 2006. www.fda.gov.

41. Rick Perry, "Statement of Gov. Rick Perry on HPV Vaccine Executive Order" news release, February 5, 2007. http://governor.state.tx.us.

42. Quoted in *Fort Bend Herald*, "Lawmakers Discuss Requiring Cervical Cancer Vaccine."

43. Concerned Women for America, "HPV: Highly Politicized Vaccine," *Family Voice*, May/June 2007, p. 7.

44. Quoted in Bevington, "Researcher Blasts HPV Marketing."

45. Quoted in Bevington, "Researcher Blasts HPV Marketing."

46. Tegan N. Millspaw, "Examining the FDA's Vaccine Records," June 30, 2008. www.judicialwatch.org.

47. Sharyl Attkisson, "Gardasil HPV Vaccine Side Effects," CBS News: Primary Source, July 8, 2008. www.cbsnews.com.

List of Illustrations

Index

age, as risk factor for HPV, 12, 30, 64

AIDS Treatment Update (journal), 14, 33, 62

Alvarez, Manny, 60

American Cancer Society, 10, 11, 52, 63

  on annual number of new genital wart diagnoses, 37

  recommendations on cervical cancer prevention, 15

  on transmission of genital HPV, 43

American Medical Association (AMA), 11, 83

  on prevalence of HPV infection, 30

Attkisson, Sharyl, 72, 73

babies, risk for HPV infection among, 40–41, 48

Bambenek, John, 75

Barnard, Jakelyn, 77

Bartholomew, Deborah A., 59

Beard, J.W., 20

Benson, Jeff, 8, 59

Binns, Corey, 21

Bishara, Rima, 76

Brown University Health Services, 45

Burcham, Heather, 70

Cain, Kelly, 58

cancers

  anal, 14, 62

  caused by HPV infection, 13–14, 56, 58, 59

    in men, 53–54

  oral, 14

    HPV types causing, 57, 62

    number of oral sex partners and risk for, 65

  skin, 61

  See also cervical cancer

Centers for Disease Control and Prevention (CDC), 13–14, 62

  on number of HIV vs. HPV infections, 22

  on prevalence of HPV infections, 19

cervical cancer, 13

  annual diagnoses/deaths from, 52, 62

  cases preventable with vaccination, 65 (chart)

  discovery of relationship between HPV infection and, 50–51

  HPV strains causing, 64

  prevalence of, 63

  rate of, by age group, 64 (chart)

Concerned Women for America (CWA), 16, 71

condoms, 46

  effectiveness at preventing HPV infection, 15–16

Daut, Arianna, 8–9

DeAngelis, Catherine D., 67

deaths

  from cervical cancer, 52, 62

  linked to HPV vaccine, 72, 81

diagnosis

  of genital warts, 15

  of warts, 14

D'Souza, Gypsyamber, 58

Ellwood, Liz, 53

Family Research Council, 71

Food and Drug Administration, U.S. (FDA), 16, 62, 72

Gardasil, 7, 68, 79, 81

About the Author

Peggy J. Parks holds a bachelor of science degree from Aquinas College in Grand Rapids, Michigan, where she graduated magna cum laude. She has written more than 70 nonfiction educational books for children and young adults, and has self-published her own cookbook called *Welcome Home: Recipes, Memories, and Traditions from the Heart.* Parks lives in Muskegon, Michigan, a town that she says inspires her writing because of its location on the shores of Lake Michigan.